Elvis Presley
Unseen Archives

Elvis Presley
Unseen Archives

Marie Clayton

p

This is a Parragon Book
This edition published in 2005

Parragon
Queen Street House
4 Queen Street
Bath, BA1 1HE, UK

Text © Parragon
For details of photographs, see pages 382–383

Produced by Atlantic Publishing
Design and origination by Cambridge Publishing Management Ltd

Cover Design by Kit Rocket

ISBN 1-40545-687-6

Printed in China

Contents

Chapter One

Love Me Tender

Playing records at June Juanico's house in
Biloxi, summer 1956.

Opposite: Music producer Sam Phillips (right)
and Bob Neal (left) standing behind Elvis as he
signs his management contract with Neal.
This was the official picture that ran in the
trades – in fact Elvis was still underage so his
parents signed for him as his legal guardians.

Previous page: Elvis at around two years old.

(the exact number is uncertain) and told his listeners it was sure to be a hit. The results stunned everybody: thousands of phone calls requested more of the new singer and, much to Sam Phillips' surprise, Elvis's music was not only popular with the white audience, but with the black one too.

At first, Scotty Moore managed the group but, later, DJ Bob Neal took over, making bookings for live appearances at clubs and concerts, and later organising local concert tours. They began to play regularly at the Eagle's Nest in Memphis, but Sam Phillips also managed to get a booking at that mecca of country singing, Nashville's Grand Ole Opry. It was unheard of for an unknown singer to play the Opry, and all of them were thrilled; unfortunately, though, the audience was not ready for their new style and Elvis was advised to stick to driving trucks. He never played there again. The Louisiana Hayride, broadcast on KWKH from Shreveport's Municipal Auditorium, proved more welcoming. Elvis and the Blue Moon Boys were an instant hit and were quickly invited back. They began to tour almost full-time – often driving all night, playing a concert then driving on to the next show, with just a few snatched hours of sleep in the back of the car. Despite this, Elvis always seemed constantly active and rarely tired; when he finally did sleep, though, it would be for 11 or 12 hours.

Now he was releasing records, and playing regularly at the Louisiana Hayride and other well-known venues, Elvis began to feel he was really on his way. He already had a large group of fans, who would arrive whenever he was due to appear. He was still a local phenomenon, however, and he needed another push to achieve national popularity. That push was not long coming – in late 1954, Elvis met Colonel Tom Parker for the first time, and he soon had plans for the still rather naive young singer who was driving audiences wild.

The Colonel had started out in carnival, but moved into showbusiness when he became the manager of singer Eddy Arnold. When he met Elvis, he was working as a promoter and his astute business practices, promotional skills and attention to detail were already famous. Although his title was an honorary one, conferred by a state governor, he insisted on using it at all times. Having arranged a few tours for Elvis, and noting the audience reaction, he began to take over, manoeuvring everyone else out of the way.

With the Colonel's help, Elvis transferred to the national stage and was soon headlining shows across the country. Women went wild as he shook his hips or jiggled his legs – movements a world away from those of other singers of the time, who hardly moved at all while they sang. Some religious leaders took exception to his 'lewd' actions onstage, and called for both Elvis and his music to be banned.

Don't call us…

The second Sun single, 'Good Rockin' Tonight' was as great a success as the first. Elvis, Scotty Moore and Bill Black soon had regular concert bookings and Sam Phillips arranged for them to appear on Nashville's Grand Ole Opry. Unfortunately the audience was more used to traditional country singers, and the response was lukewarm. Afterwards, the show's talent coordinator, Jim Denny, suggested Elvis should go back to driving a truck.

In August 1956, Elvis began work on his first film, *Love Me Tender*, a drama set just after the Civil War. Elvis played the youngest son of a farming family, who marries the girlfriend of his eldest brother after everyone assumes that the brother is dead. When the older brother returns, the family is torn apart and Elvis's character is killed. The film co-starred Debra Paget and Richard Egan; Elvis appears again at the end, singing the title song over the credits. The Colonel was astute enough to retain the publishing rights to the film's score, rather than handing them over to the studio and, after Elvis appeared on *The Ed Sullivan Show*, advance orders of two million were received for the single 'Love Me Tender'. The film opened in 500 theatres that November, and was a huge hit despite an unenthusiastic response from the movie critics.

The Colonel was also quick to realise the potential for Elvis-related merchandise, and set up companies to sell a Presley product range that included jeans, charm bracelets, stick-on sideburns, hair pomade, bubblegum cards and even lipstick. At the centre of all this fuss, however, Elvis was becoming increasingly isolated, his movements restricted, and was already beginning to lay down the roots of the lifestyle that would eventually lead to his destruction.

Elvis appeared for the first time on the Louisiana Hayride in October 1954. This time the performance went down very well and he and the Blue Moon Boys were soon given a contract to appear every Saturday night. The Hayride was broadcast live from the Municipal Auditorium in Shreveport, and reached 28 states; it was much more innovative than the Opry and became a haven for new talent.

The Hillbilly Cat…

Elvis takes a turn at the drums. At first, he was backed on stage only by Scotty on lead guitar and Bill on bass, but after they decided to hire a full-time drummer they were joined by DJ Fontana. As a musician, Elvis was largely self-taught. His parents did not have the money to pay for lessons, but he grew up surrounded by music and quickly learned to carry a tune.

Accomplished pianist

Although he rarely played in public, Elvis was also an accomplished pianist. He usually played for himself or close friends, and only when he felt happy and at ease. He often played gospel music for pleasure and thought about becoming a gospel singer, but rockabilly – the early form of rock 'n' roll – was what the audience wanted.

Lifelong friends

Elvis first appeared in Las Vegas in April 1956, but the engagement was not a great success. However, he met Liberace there for the first time and the two of them went on to become lifelong friends.

Heartbreak Hotel

Released in 1956, 'Heartbreak Hotel' was the first Elvis record that became a hit for RCA. Elvis had first heard the song in 1955 at a disc jockey convention and had immediately decided he wanted to record it. Songwriters Mae Axton and Tommy Durden had written the song after reading a newspaper article about a young man who had committed suicide, leaving a note that said, 'I walk a lonely street'. The song was very different from the material Elvis had previously recorded, but it went on to become the first of his records to sell a million copies and his first No. 1 hit.

King meets queen

Irish McCalla, the star of *Sheena, Queen of the Jungle*, holds Elvis hostage. The two of them appeared together on *The Milton Berle Show* in spring 1956.

Speculating about romance

Judy Powell Spreckels, former wife of sugar heir Adolph Spreckels, manages to catch Elvis after *The Milton Berle Show*. The two of them exchanged rings, and the press speculated that they were enjoying a romance.

Opposite: The Milton Berle Show that featured Elvis's first appearance was broadcast from the deck of the USS *Hancock*, which was docked at the San Diego Naval Station. Despite the novelty of the location, it was his second appearance on the show in June of that year that brought more publicity.

Hound Dog

During his second appearance on *The Milton Berle Show*, Elvis sang 'Hound Dog' for the first time on television. It was a new song, but the audience loved it and Elvis responded to their enthusiasm by taking his hip-swivelling performance to greater heights. 'Hound Dog' was released in July 1956 and sold over 5 million copies by the end of the year.

Topping the ratings

As he reached the final part of 'Hound Dog', Elvis slowed down the tempo of the song and proceeded to thrust his hips in time to the music in a distinctly suggestive way. The studio audience were driven to a frenzy of excitement, screaming and laughing at the same time. That evening, for the first time in the season, *The Milton Berle Show* topped *Sergeant Bilko* in the ratings.

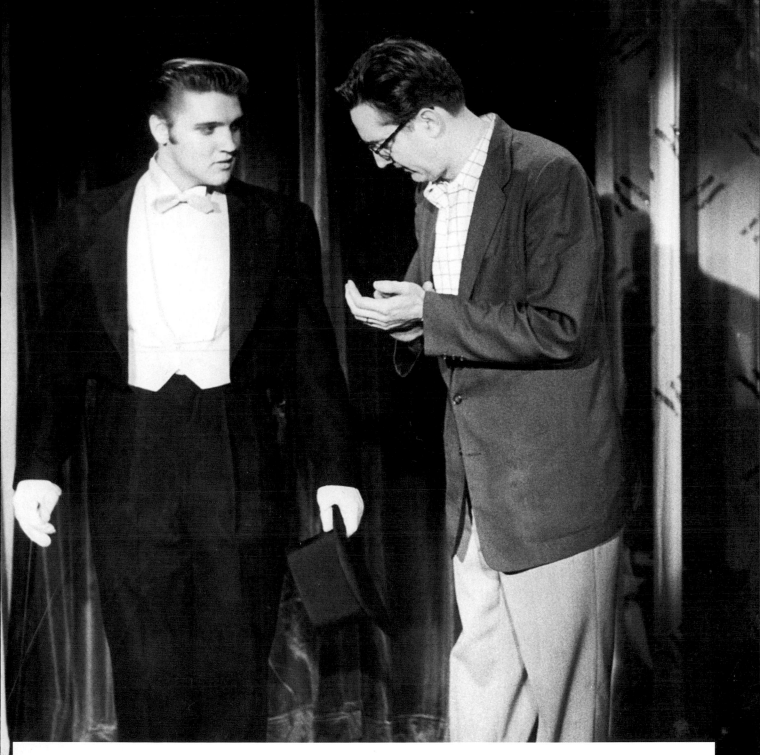

Fans furious at critics' response

Soon afterwards Elvis appeared on the *Steve Allen Show*, but Allen insisted his performance be toned down and that he should wear a tuxedo. The fans were furious, and picketed the NBC studios the following morning.

Opposite: The day after *The Milton Berle Show* was broadcast, many critics condemned Elvis's performance. John Crosby of the *New York Herald Tribune* said he was 'unspeakably untalented and vulgar', Jack O'Brian of the New York Journal-American wrote of '…a display of primitive physical movement difficult to describe in terms suitable to a family newspaper…', and Ben Gross said in the Daily News that '…he gave an exhibition that was suggestive and vulgar, tinged with the kind of animalism that should be confined to dives and bordellos.'

A new, confident Elvis

On stage at Russwood Park, in July 1956. When Elvis first appeared, dressed all in black except for red socks and tie, the fans rushed out of their seats and swept forwards towards the stage. The last few months had given Elvis a new confidence, so he was able to tease and control the crowd without letting anything get out of hand.

Time out for Mum and Dad

Top: Elvis takes time out to have a few words with his mother, Gladys, and father, Vernon.

Bottom: The Colonel always had a supply of photographs for the fans to buy – and Elvis was happy to sign them. In later years, he rarely went out in public because he was constantly mobbed by his fans.

Hollywood, here I come

In August 1956, filming began on Elvis's first movie, *Love Me Tender*, which was being made by Twentieth-Century Fox. After his screen test for Hal Wallis, Elvis had been offered a three-picture deal by Paramount – but they had no suitable vehicle for him, so had loaned him to Twentieth-Century Fox. Elvis had an excellent memory, and he not only knew his own part before he arrived in Hollywood, but had also learned the entire script by heart. His co-stars were Richard Egan and Debra Paget, both experienced actors, and Elvis was very nervous but also extremely willing to learn. The producer, David Weisbart, had produced *Rebel Without a Cause* and Elvis was excited to meet him as he had deeply admired James Dean.

Down on the farm...

Originally entitled *The Reno Brothers*, *Love Me Tender* was a drama, set just after the Civil War. Elvis played the youngest son of a farming family, who marries the girlfriend of his eldest brother after everyone assumes that the brother is dead. When the older brother returns, the family is torn apart and Elvis's character is killed. Since the producers worried that the fans would be upset if their idol died, an alternative ending was shot, in which he survives. In the end they stayed with the original storyline, but Elvis appears again at the end, singing the title song over the credits.

Love Me Tender: a million orders

The theme song, 'Love Me Tender', was based on a Civil War ballad called 'Aura Lee'. Elvis was better known for more raunchy numbers, but he sang the ballad with real feeling. When it was released in September 1956 as a single the song was a great hit, so the name of the film was quickly changed to *Love Me Tender* before it was released. This was the only film in which Elvis appeared where the part was not specifically written for him – in fact Robert Wagner was originally under consideration to play the role.

Time revealed that RCA had record-breaking advance orders of one million for the single, and even before the movie opened the record reached No. 1 in the *Billboard* Top 100.

Natural acting ability

Producer David Weisbart told reporters that Elvis had the same smouldering appeal for teenagers, and the same impulsive nature, as James Dean. He advised Elvis not to have acting lessons but to rely on his greatest asset – his natural ability.

Opposite top: Debra Paget played the elder brother's girlfriend in *Love Me Tender*. Elvis had a big crush on her, but she did not return his regard – although she thought he was 'very sweet'.

Opposite bottom: Although *Love Me Tender* had only four musical numbers, they were carefully worked into the storyline.

Charming the birds
from the trees…

Elvis was well-liked by his co-stars, and they went out of their way to help him in the new and strange world of movie-making. Richard Egan, who played the elder brother, said of him later, 'That boy could charm the birds from the trees'.

Director Robert Webb was very patient with his fledgling star, taking him aside between shots to go over the scenes and breaking the lines down to show the emphasis.

Back home in Tupelo

Nick Adams, an actor and Hollywood hustler who had become Elvis's friend, introduced him to Natalie Wood. The papers reported that Elvis and Natalie were having a sizzling romance, but they usually went around in a gang with Nick and his other friends. Natalie described Elvis as 'a real pixie… he has a wonderful little-boy quality'.

Opposite: In September, Elvis appeared at a homecoming concert back in Tupelo. Before the concert began a parade was held in his honour, but the Colonel vetoed the suggestion that Elvis should ride in it because of concerns over security. Main Street was decked with a giant banner that said, 'Tupelo Welcomes Elvis Presley Home'. Elvis's parents, Vernon and Gladys, were there to see his triumph – though Gladys later told a friend that it had made her uncomfortable to remember how poor they had been when they lived there.

He wore Blue Velvet

For the concert, Elvis wore a heavy blue velvet shirt that Natalie Wood had had made for him by her own tailor – despite the fact that it was a very hot day. He teased the crowd, walking close to the edge of the stage and leaning down so the fans could just touch his fingers. One time he misjudged the distance, and lost one of the silver buttons from his shirt.

During the concert, Tupelo mayor James Ballard gave Elvis the key to the city and Mississippi governor JP Coleman came on stage to praise 'America's number-one entertainer'.

On second thoughts…

Ed Sullivan discusses a few points with Elvis during preparations for his second appearance on *The Ed Sullivan Show* in October 1956. Although Sullivan had declared that Elvis would never appear on his show, he later backed down and signed him for three performances. Elvis was paid a total of $50,000 for his appearances – which was considerably more than the sum the Colonel had originally asked for when he first approached Sullivan and had been turned down. When the first show was broadcast in early September, actor Charles Laughton acted as host since Sullivan was recovering from a car accident.

Fooling with Bill Black

While Elvis played to the girls, Bill Black often played the fool with his bass in the background. Sometimes he pretended to dance with it, at others he rode it like horse – which always elicited a laugh from the audience. The ratings for the *Sullivan Show* – and every other show – invariably went up when Elvis appeared.

Hear no evil…

Rehearsing for *The Ed Sullivan Show*. By this time Elvis appeared relaxed and confident.

Opposite: Despite all the controversy, Elvis enjoyed appearing before an audience, along with Scotty Moore, DJ Fontana on drums, and Bill Black on bass. At the end of Elvis's third appearance on his show, Ed Sullivan told the audience that he thought Elvis was 'a real decent fine boy'.

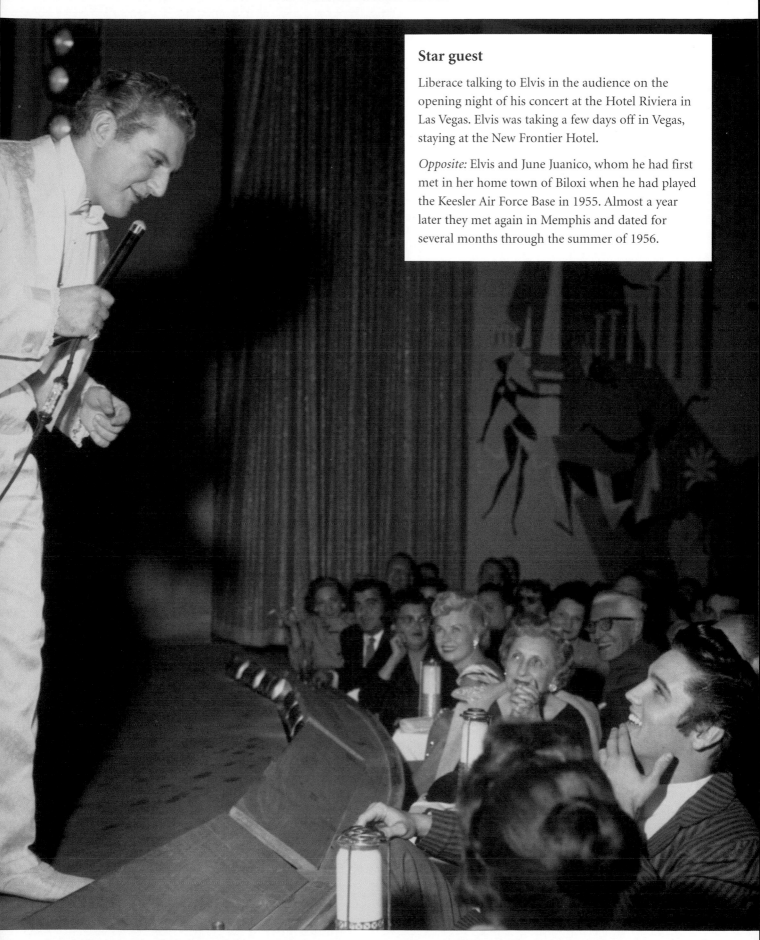

Star guest

Liberace talking to Elvis in the audience on the opening night of his concert at the Hotel Riviera in Las Vegas. Elvis was taking a few days off in Vegas, staying at the New Frontier Hotel.

Opposite: Elvis and June Juanico, whom he had first met in her home town of Biloxi when he had played the Keesler Air Force Base in 1955. Almost a year later they met again in Memphis and dated for several months through the summer of 1956.

Just pure gold

After the concert, Liberace and Elvis swopped jackets and instruments and fooled around for the cameras. Liberace's jacket was a gold cutaway, and was the inspiration for the famous $2,500 gold-lamé suit that the Colonel had made up for Elvis by Nudie Cohen the following year. Liberace told journalists, 'Elvis and I may be characters – but we can afford to be.' Elvis always sent flowers for Liberace's opening nights.

November 1956

When *Love Me Tender* was released in November 1956, a huge cut-out of Elvis as Clint Reno was unveiled on a New York City theatre. Thousands of fans turned out to see the movie – despite the fact that the critics' reviews of Elvis's performance were derisive and condescending. The reviews were hardly surprising, given the bad publicity Elvis had been getting throughout the year, but they were very unfair. For an inexperienced actor, Elvis acquitted himself very well.

A casual, windswept Elvis. By the end of 1956, he had come a long way. His records were now in the charts, he had a nationwide following of fans and had made his first Hollywood movie, which was a big box office success. Despite all the adulation, most people agree that in terms of his character he had changed very little. He was still unfailing polite and charming to everyone he met, and he still went home to his parents whenever he had the opportunity. However, the obsessive behaviour of the fans was becoming an increasing problem – Elvis could hardly walk down the street without getting besieged by adoring admirers.

Car-crazy…

Below: The former truck driver studies the engine of something a little more powerful. Throughout his life Elvis had a fascination for cars and he not only bought many for himself, he also often bought them as gifts for friends, acquaintances – and even total strangers. The first car he ever owned was a 1941 Lincoln coupé, bought by Vernon and Gladys. When he first began to earn serious money he bought his mother a brand new pink Cadillac – even though she did not drive.

Left: A relaxed Elvis in front of the camera.

ENITENTIARY
PERSONEL
CAPT 9
CMLIAN 165
TOTAL 421
INMATE
PEN 2660
ADOL 186
TRIAL 42
PEN 2889
TOTAL 3082

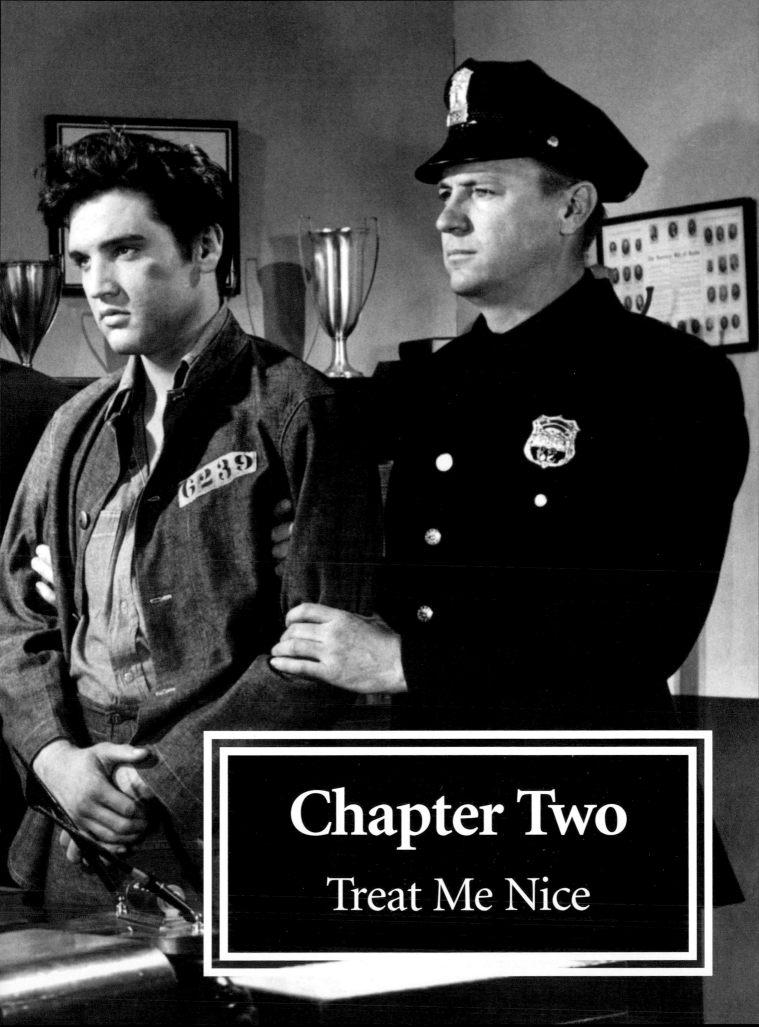

Chapter Two

Treat Me Nice

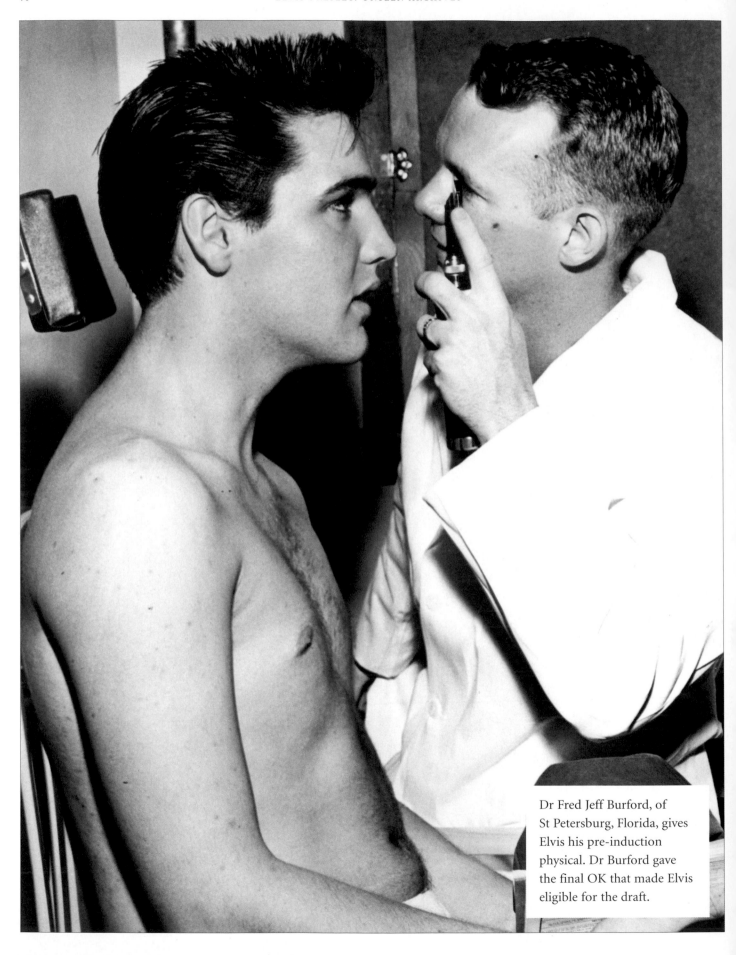

Dr Fred Jeff Burford, of
St Petersburg, Florida, gives
Elvis his pre-induction
physical. Dr Burford gave
the final OK that made Elvis
eligible for the draft.

By the beginning of 1957, Elvis was accompanied by armed security guards wherever he went, since he could no longer so much as step into the street without being mobbed by fans, causing a riot. He was constantly surrounded by members of his entourage, a close-knit circle of men who were both companions and support group. They fuelled his ego, rushed to fulfil every whim, and were on hand 24 hours a day to sing gospel or to party. Often badly behaved, they appeared arrogant to outsiders, and they soon became known in most circles as the 'Memphis Mafia'.

After Elvis had played a concert, he and the Mafia would usually party all night with local musicians – and plenty of girls too. To relax, he sang gospel music or played the piano. He could now afford to buy whatever he wanted to eat – but had a weakness for junk food, particularly cheeseburgers, sliced banana and peanut butter sandwiches, greasy doughnuts, crisply burnt bacon, fried or mashed potatoes and dark-brown gravy. A diet of this kind of food was beginning to cause weight problems – although he was still burning off a great many calories in nervous energy. He also often walked in his sleep when he was anxious or upset, which gave those around him cause for concern about his safety. During the unhappy booking at the New Frontier Hotel in Las Vegas in 1956, his companion Red West regularly sat up all night in case Elvis walked straight out of the open window.

Despite Elvis's burgeoning health problems, the hours spent on the road, the constant lack of sleep and his poor diet, he always seemed to find plenty of energy when it was time to take the stage.

For some time, rumours had been spreading that Elvis was about to be drafted. Early in 1957 he reported to the Kennedy Veterans Hospital in Memphis for his pre-induction US Army physical; he was classed 1-A and therefore eligible for military service, although the authorities said it was unlikely he would be called within the next six months. The Army also confirmed that the famous hair – Elvis's pride and joy – would have to come off. Meanwhile, there was another film to be made, *Loving You*, about a singer in search of fame. It also starred Lizbeth Scott and Wendell Corey – established actors who would not feel the need to eclipse the new kid on the block. Gladys and Vernon came to visit their son on-set and were filmed for one scene, watching the concert that takes place at the climax of the story.

One of the first major purchases Elvis had made with his new-found wealth was a home for his parents, in Audubon Drive, Memphis. Unfortunately, fans often turned up in their hundreds to hang around outside, and the neighbours soon tired of this constant intrusion. Elvis decided he needed a property with some seclusion, so Vernon and Gladys set out to find one. As soon as they saw Graceland they fell in love with it, and quickly called Elvis to come and see it for himself. A Georgian colonial-style mansion, Graceland had been built in 1939 for Dr Thomas Moore and his wife, and named after Mrs Moore's great aunt Grace, who had owned the land. It was set in 13.75 acres of grounds, and placed well back from Highway 51 – later to be renamed Elvis Presley Boulevard. Elvis was immediately enthusiastic about the property, and the purchase was completed within a week. Renovations were soon under way, as well as essential structural repairs. Elvis had a swimming pool added, and installed a real soda fountain and specially made gates with a musical note motif. He had the interior entirely redecorated, mostly in dark colours with glitzy touches. Over the years, further additions included a recording studio, a 40-foot trophy room, stables, fenced-in fields and vegetable gardens.

In trouble…

Top: Elvis got himself into trouble when he was accused of pulling a gun on a Private First Class Hershel, after the young Marine claimed Elvis had insulted his wife. Since Elvis had never met Mrs Hershel – and the gun was a prop, which he had brought back from Hollywood – the whole affair was settled out of court.

Bottom: In a still from his third movie, *Jailhouse Rock*, Elvis plays Vince Everett, who is sent to prison for killing a man in self-defence. His character is hot-blooded and bitter over the unfair sentence, and becomes an angry, sullen and brooding young man. The fans are therefore treated to several scenes of a very passionate and provocative Elvis.

Opposite: Jailhouse Rock was a low-budget movie shot in black and white, with stylised sets, but the simple settings enhanced the serious storyline. Many believe it was one of the best movies Elvis ever made – and it made a great deal of money for MGM and for Elvis himself, who received a large percentage of the profits.

1957: Jailhouse Rock

For the big dance sequence performed to the title song, Elvis was backed by a team of professional dancers. He had initially been wary about the whole idea, but choreographer Alex Romero watched Elvis move around naturally when he was singing, and then worked the steps up into a routine. Elvis was much more comfortable and enthusiastic with the final result, and it looks very like the way he normally moved on stage. The single 'Jailhouse Rock'/'Treat Me Nice' was also a great success and sold over 3 million copies in 12 months in the US. It was the first Elvis record to reach No. 1 in the charts in Britain.

True love in the movies

Judy Tyler, as Peggy van Alden, watches Vince during one of the scenes from *Jailhouse Rock*. Peggy is the record promoter who helps Vince to stardom and falls in love with him – but haughtily refuses to respond to his advances until he becomes a reformed man.

Devastated by Judy's death

Elvis and Judy were great friends
during the shooting of the movie
– but Judy was newly married
and not interested in romance.
A few weeks after shooting
finished, she and her husband
were killed in a car accident.
Elvis was devastated and did not
attend the movie's premiere.

Parting is such sweet sorrow…

Anita Wood hugs Elvis goodbye, as he prepares to leave on a whirlwind tour of the Pacific northwest. Anita was a former beauty queen, who was now appearing on *Top Ten Dance Party* on WHBQ. She had just won the Mid-South Hollywood Star Hunt and was also about to leave, for the finalists' competition in New Orleans. The two of them were together for several years – although that didn't stop Elvis from dating a number of other women during the same period.

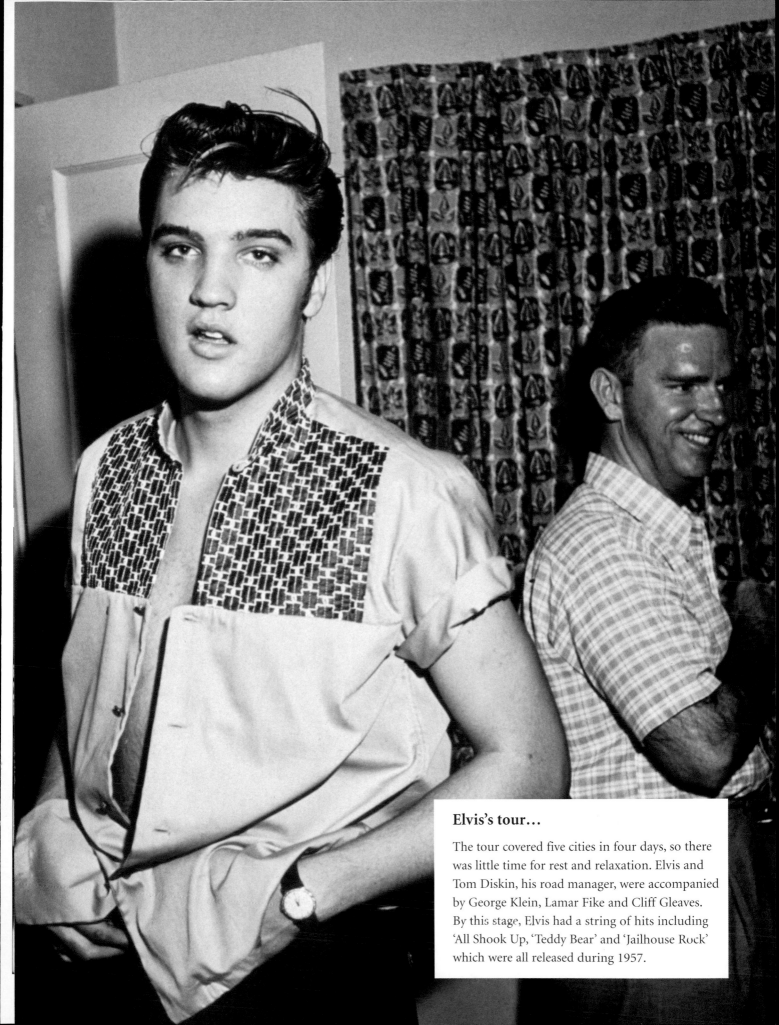

Elvis's tour…

The tour covered five cities in four days, so there was little time for rest and relaxation. Elvis and Tom Diskin, his road manager, were accompanied by George Klein, Lamar Fike and Cliff Gleaves. By this stage, Elvis had a string of hits including 'All Shook Up', 'Teddy Bear' and 'Jailhouse Rock' which were all released during 1957.

A professional touch…

During the filming of *Jailhouse Rock*
Elvis became friendly with professional
dancer Russ Tamblyn, who gave him a
few tips to sharpen up his dancing style.

Screaming and swooning

The fans now made so much noise during the concerts that no one could hear Elvis sing. They even screamed and swooned while just watching him on the screen.

Below: The Memphis premiere of *Jailhouse Rock* was held in the cinema where Elvis had once worked briefly as an usher.

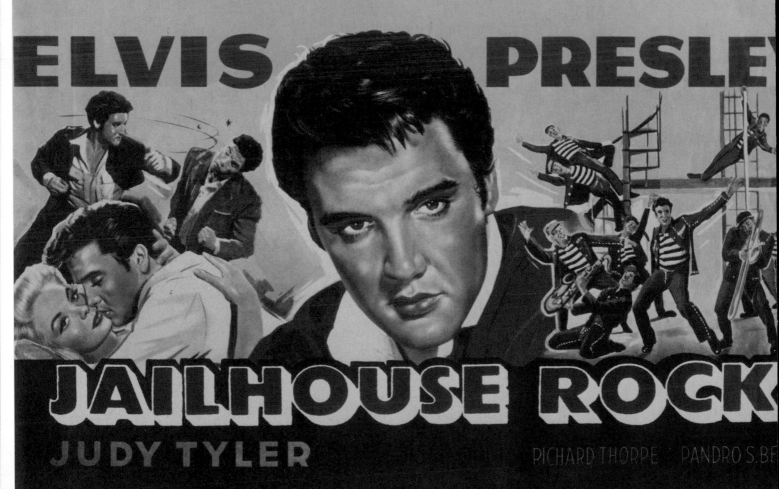

ELVIS PRESLEY

JAILHOUSE ROCK

JUDY TYLER

RICHARD THORPE · PANDRO S. BE

Drafted!

Just before Christmas 1957, Elvis received his draft notification and although he collected the notice himself to avoid publicity, the press soon got wind of it. He told reporters that he was happy the situation was finally resolved and that he was happy to return something to the country that had given him so much. When photographers wanted to picture him with the notice a minor panic ensued, as Elvis couldn't remember where he had put it.

Chapter Three

It's Now or Never

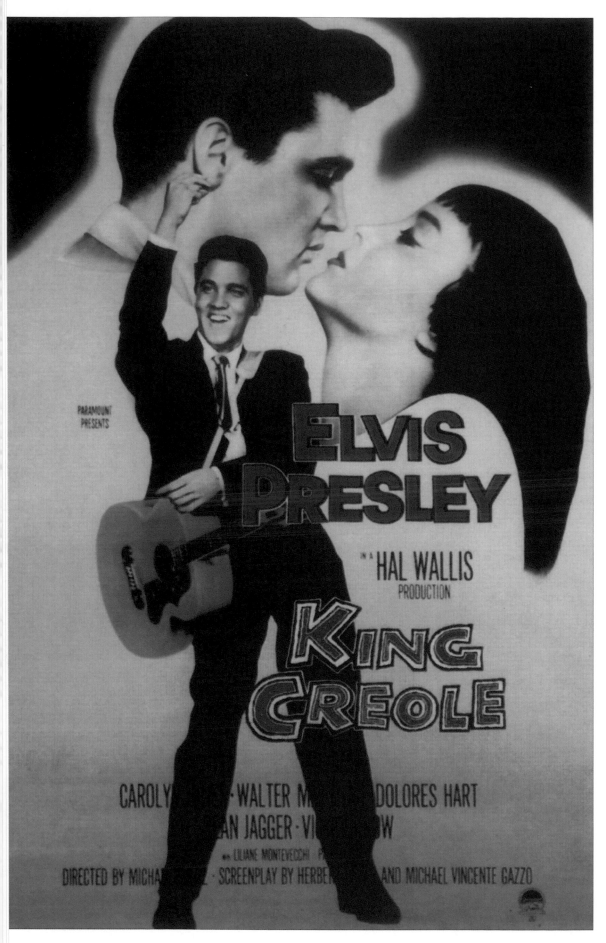

March 1958: You're in the Army now…

Opposite: Major Elbert P Turner swears Elvis into the Army at the draft board in Memphis, Tennessee. The new recruit told reporters that he was dreading the haircut he would get the following day, but that he hoped he would be treated the same as everyone else.

Left: Elvis's induction into the Army had been deferred so he could complete filming on *King Creole*. The story was of a young singer, Danny Fisher – played by Elvis – who is offered a job by a local mobster – played by Walter Matthau. Danny is a great success – but things go badly wrong when he becomes romantically involved with the mobster's girlfriend. With top production values and respected director Michael Curtiz, the movie earned Elvis his best reviews so far. The soundtrack for *King Creole* included two of Elvis's legendary songs, 'Hard Headed Woman' and 'Trouble'.

Leaving Memphis

Opposite: As the bus leaves Memphis for Fort Chaffee, Arkansas, a sad group of women watch Elvis go – including his current girlfriend, Anita Wood (centre). Press from around the world are on hand to record the entire proceedings and they follow the bus as it sets off.

Many of Elvis's loyal female fans turn up to tell him they will not forget him while he is away, and Elvis happily chats to them and signs autographs. The press are constantly present with the Army's permission – although when one photographer hides in the barracks at Fort Chaffee to try and get a picture of Elvis sleeping in his bunk, it is decided that things have gone too far and the hapless snapper is thrown out.

Shot three times

The new-look Elvis faces the cameras. All the publicity surrounding the event got Elvis so flustered that he forgot to pay the barber his 65 cent fee, and had to be called back – much to his embarrassment.

Opposite: The Army shoots Elvis three times, when he gets his jabs for typhoid, tetanus and Asian flu. As well as medical tests and a haircut, he also had to do five hours of aptitude tests and sit through a two-hour lecture on a private's rights and privileges.

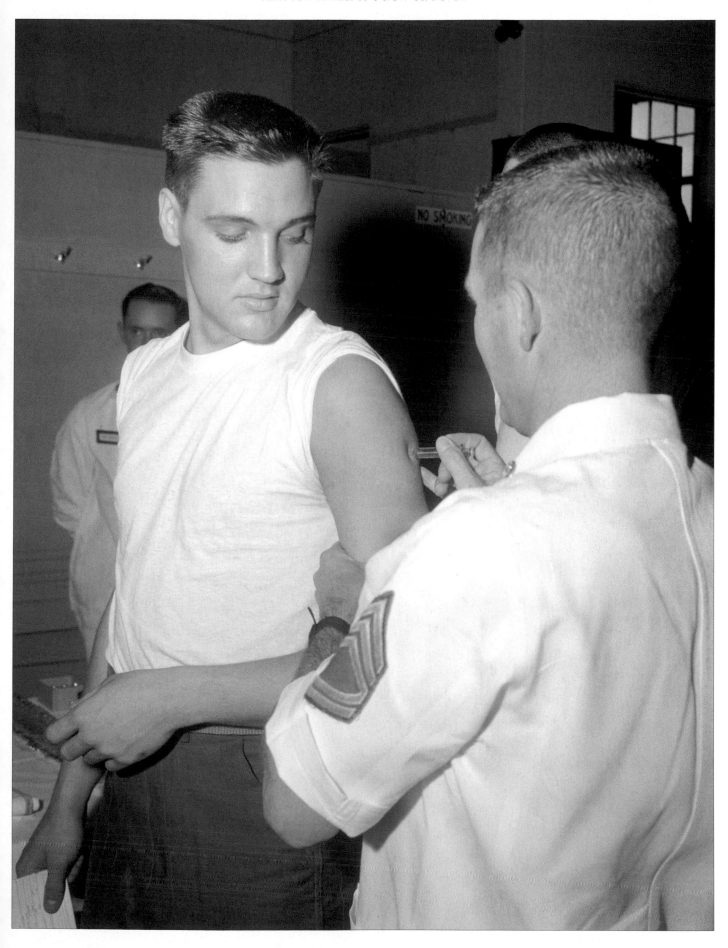

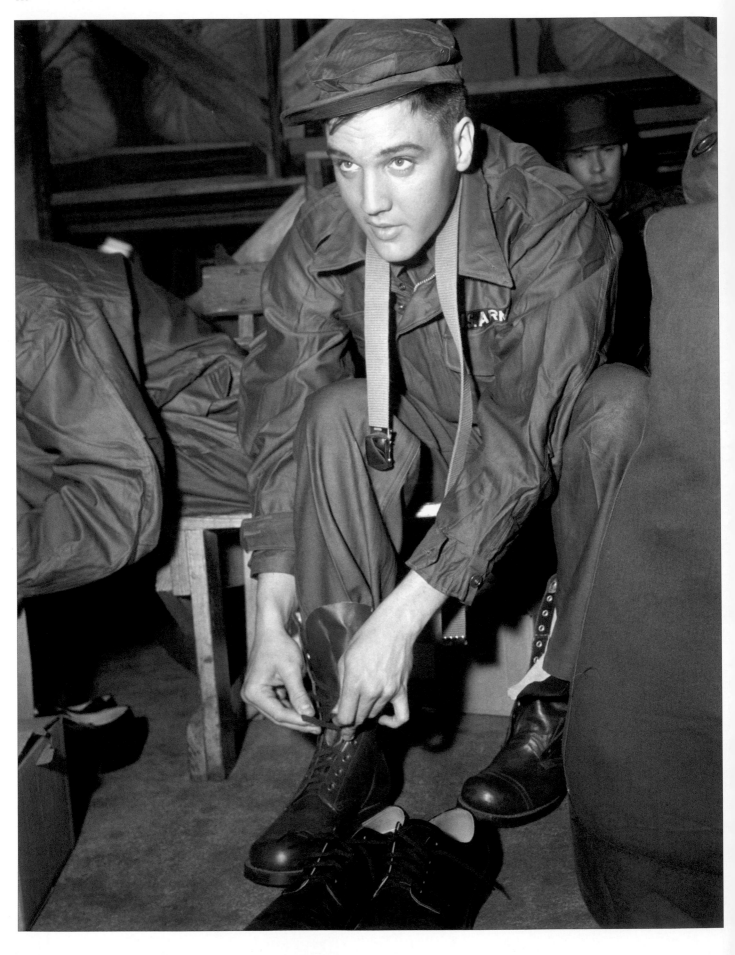

Fitted out for service

Opposite: Elvis tries on some snappy footwear and displays the latest design in Army fatigues. He dealt with all the press attention with great patience and good humour, only refusing to sign autographs while he was 'in ranks'.

It was soon announced that Elvis was to be assigned to the 2nd Armoured Division at Fort Hood just outside Killeen in Texas, to do his basic training and advanced tank instruction. The 2nd Armoured was General George Patton's famous 'Hell on Wheels' outfit. Six of the other Memphis draftees were also to be sent to Fort Hood, where basic training would last for eight weeks. There was no sign of the press attention letting up, so the Army was beginning to re-think its policy of full access.

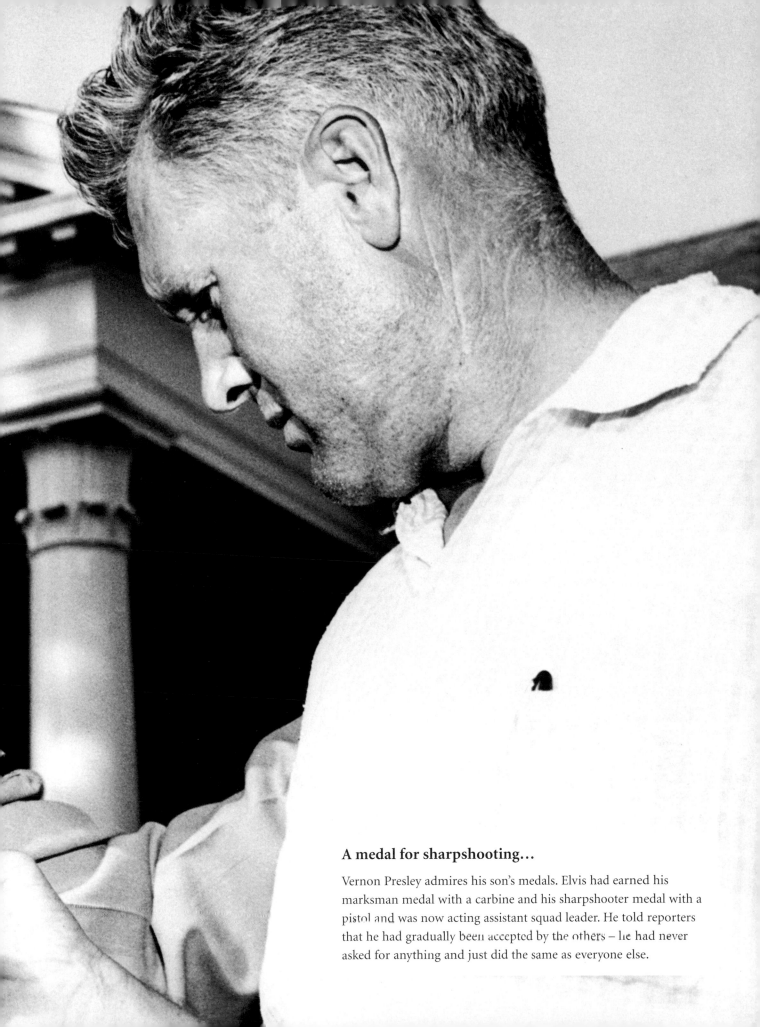

A medal for sharpshooting…

Vernon Presley admires his son's medals. Elvis had earned his marksman medal with a carbine and his sharpshooter medal with a pistol and was now acting assistant squad leader. He told reporters that he had gradually been accepted by the others – he had never asked for anything and just did the same as everyone else.

Sneaking a preview

Left: During his leave, Elvis and his parents attended a sneak preview of *King Creole*, which was held in Memphis.

Below: Elvis was always happy to come down to the gates of Graceland to sign autographs and chat to the fans. When reporters asked him why he was wearing his uniform while on leave, he replied 'I'm kinda proud of it.' He also told them that he had adjusted to Army hours and was now having trouble staying awake after midnight.

Just visiting

Anita Wood smiles for photographers as she boards a plane to Texas. She was off to visit Elvis now he had returned to base. She stayed with Sergeant Norwood and his wife at their home on the base.

August 1958: Elvis mourns his mother

Below: In August 1958, Gladys Presley was admitted to hospital. The diagnosis was uncertain, but her illness was serious enough for Elvis to be given compassionate leave. He went straight to the hospital, where Vernon was already staying – sleeping in a folding cot next to the hospital bed. His visit seemed to cheer Gladys up and for a time the doctors thought she might recover.

Opposite: In the early hours of Thursday morning Gladys died of a heart attack. When reporters turned up at Graceland later in the day, they found Vernon and Elvis sitting on the steps of the house. Elvis, sobbing uncontrollably, told them that his mother was all they had lived for and that she had always been his 'best girl'.

September '58: Off over the sea

Just over a week after the funeral Elvis had to return to Fort Hood to complete his basic training and a month later his unit left for Germany. Since 125 newsmen had arrived in New York to see him off, a press conference and photo opportunity were organised before he boarded the ship. His kit had already been loaded, so a borrowed duffel bag was quickly provided for the pictures.

Below: Although Elvis had never been in Europe, he already had fans there. At least 500 German teenagers arrived to welcome him when the ship docked at Bremerhaven. From the docks the soldiers caught a train to the base at Friedberg, near Frankfurt. Elvis waved to fans and to waiting newsmen as the train left the station.

In Germany

Elvis poses in his dress
uniform in Germany. At first
he was hounded by
photographers and bothered
constantly by other soldiers
looking for autographs, but
the press were soon banned
from the base and the other
soldiers got used to his
presence, so things settled
down into a routine.

Margit dates her 'very nice boy'

Elvis holding hands with Margit Buergin, a young typist with an electrical supply company in Frankfurt. She had waited outside his hotel to get his autograph and photographers had called for them to kiss. Elvis happily obliged, and he dated Margit several times afterwards. She was only sixteen, but looked older, and still lived with her mother. She told the press that she thought Elvis was 'a very nice boy' and that she liked him very much.

Rocking with Bill Haley in Frankfurt

Bill Haley was appearing in Frankfurt on 23 October and in Stuttgart six days later. Elvis went to see him both times, although he had to stay backstage during the show to avoid causing a riot. He told Haley that he was grateful for his help and encouragement in the early days – and that, without it, he might still be driving a truck.

On manoeuvres

Elvis was assigned to Company C, a scout platoon, where he drove a jeep for Reconnaissance Platoon Sergeant Ira Jones. One reason that Company C was selected was because it spent much of its time on manoeuvres, which would keep Private Presley well out of the public eye.

One of the boys

Elvis shaving at base camp in Grafenwöhr while on manoeuvres. It was a cold, dismal and muddy place near the border, but Elvis endured the same conditions as the other soldiers and turned out to be resourceful and clever scout. He proved himself not only to his platoon sergeant but also to his fellow soldiers and was finally accepted by them as one of the boys. While he was away, Vernon met Dee Stanley – who had been trying to persuade Elvis to come to dinner with her family – and the two of them became close. Dee later divorced her Army husband and married Vernon, much to Elvis's disapproval.

The day after Elvis returned from manoeuvres, he took possession of a
second-hand white BMW 507 sports car that had previously been used
by German racer Hans Stuck for demonstrations. At a photo call, the
keys were handed over by a pretty model. He had also bought an old
Cadillac for his father to use and a Volkswagen Beetle for the boys. The
first Christmas in Germany was sad for everyone, not only because they
were away from home but because it was the first without Gladys.

Opposite: Elvis demonstrates the equipment
in his jeep to four-year-old Michael Jones,
the son of his platoon sergeant, at an Open
House held at the 3rd Armoured Division
headquarters in Friedberg in April 1959.

All teamwork but no touring

During the time he was in Germany, Elvis never once appeared on stage or sang for a proper audience. He had been instructed not to do so by Colonel Tom Parker – partly so that he would not be treated differently, but also partly because the Colonel did not see why the Army should get for free what everyone else was prepared to pay a fortune for. Back home, the Colonel was using Elvis's absence and the shortage of material to up the ante in all his negotiations with RCA and the Hollywood studios.

Above: When a World War I memorial in a German village had to be moved to a new location, the US Army stepped in to help. Private Presley directed operations as the sections were lifted by crane. Later he told the press that he thought he and the other soldiers had worked pretty well as a team.

Sergeant Presley is no richer

Opposite: The advancement in rank carried no increase in pay, but since Elvis was considerably richer than most soldiers, this did not concern him!

Below: While he was in Germany, Elvis did not live on base with the other soldiers. His family and a couple of the Memphis Mafia were there with him and at first they stayed in a series of hotels. After a shaving cream fight and an incident when a small fire set off all the alarms, they were asked to move out, so Elvis rented a house at Goethestrasse 14. Here his grandmother was able to cook the kind of food he liked – and Elvis was often able to slip back home for lunch.

Colonel Parker holds the fort

The whole time Elvis was away, the Colonel kept his name in the public eye by judicious release of the material available. He also made sure the fan clubs were kept informed and sent out over four thousand telegrams and messages to fellow performers on his and Elvis's behalf. At a time when the industry was in a slump, he managed to keep Elvis on top. Here he gets a little extra publicity by presenting a whole ham to a state governor.

Elvis in Paris

Left: The Army was not all mud and guns – here Elvis enjoys a few days R&R in Paris, where he stayed in the Prince de Galles in Avenue Georges V with Lamar Fike, Charlie Hodge and Rex Mansfield. They visited famous nightclubs such as the Moulin Rouge and the Folies Bergère and once took the entire chorus line of Bluebell girls from the Lido back to their hotel. They had so much fun in Paris that Elvis decided to stay one more night, paying for a limousine to drive them all back to Friedberg the following day.

Below: Then it was back to active service again.

A snowy homecoming

Sergeant Elvis Presley carries his bags through the snow, after arriving in New Jersey from Germany in March 1960. He was transferred to Fort Dix, where he stayed for 48 hours until he was officially discharged.

Opposite top: Back in Germany Priscilla is pictured with her photograph of Elvis as she writes him a letter. All the papers referred to her as his 16-year-old girlfriend, but at the time she was still only 14 – although she was very mature for her age. Her family had insisted on meeting Elvis before they would let her see him regularly, but were won over by his charm and sincerity.

Opposite bottom: The press were on hand again to record every step of the discharge proceedings. Here Elvis boards a bus at Fort Dix that will take him from his orientation lecture to the base finance building to collect his final pay.

March 1960: Parker's 'boy' is back

Opposite: Colonel Parker looks on as Elvis waves to fans. He had carefully orchestrated all the details of the homecoming, making sure that the fans were around to give Elvis the kind of welcome he deserved – and prove once and for all that Elvis was still on top.

Above: At a press conference, Elvis wore a specially-tailored formal dress uniform – but the tailor had made a mistake with the stripes. The extra rocker on the shoulder designated a rank of staff sergeant, but Elvis had only made sergeant. Some reporters accepted it was a mistake – the more cynical blamed the Colonel for trying to build up the reputation of 'his boy'.

Back to work – and play

Above: Lucky fan Barbara Ann Murray of Roselle Park, New Jersey, gets to sit on Elvis's lap and receives a kiss.

Right: Actress Tina Louise, who went on to become the star of *Gilligan's Island*, interviews Elvis for the cameras.

Opposite: With his hair already beginning to grow out of the regulation Army haircut, Elvis was beginning to look more like the King of Rock 'n' Roll again. He told reporters that he planned to rest at home – although in fact he had a busy schedule. He not only had a recording session planned, but also an appearance on the Frank Sinatra Show and was soon to start shooting on a new film. Instead he told the newsmen about his newfound interest in karate, which he had been studying in Germany.

Welcome home, Elvis

Also on hand to greet the homecoming star was Nancy Sinatra, who presented him with a gift from her father. They were soon linked romantically – although the relationship never appeared very serious on either side.

Opposite: After collecting an autograph, Barbara Ann Murray gives Elvis a welcome home hug.

March 1960: Official discharge

After being officially discharged, Elvis signs
a few autographs for his Army buddies.

Opposite: Elvis shows the waiting newsmen
his certificate of discharge and the contents
of his last pay packet.

Priscilla: the girl he left behind

Priscilla consoles herself by playing Elvis records back in Germany. She was delighted when he did keep his promise to stay in touch, and soon he was making plans to bring her over to America.

Above: The Colonel reminds Elvis not to forget his commission – and Elvis hands him the entire $109.54.

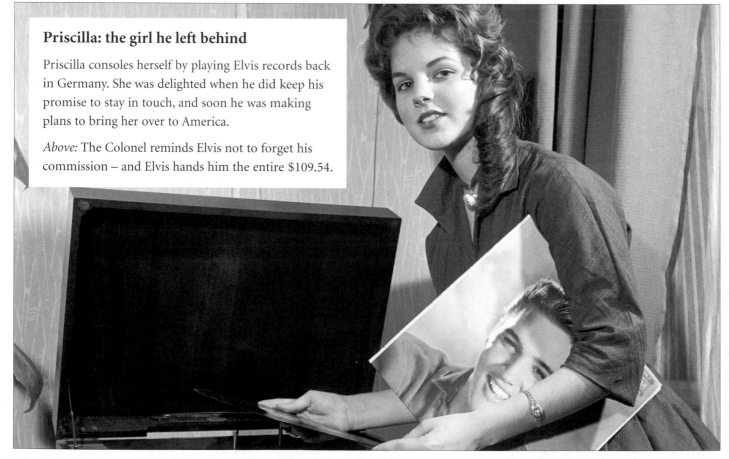

A duet with Frank

Elvis's appearance on the *Frank Sinatra Show* indicated a change of direction. Perfectly dressed and incredibly elegant in a tuxedo, he sang two songs with professional aplomb, and then did a duet with Sinatra himself. Although some fans mourned the passing of the hell-raising Elvis, most agreed that he had matured and loved the new style.

Elvis, we still love you!

On his train journey down to Miami to record the Sinatra show, almost the entire route was lined with fans and press. Of course the Colonel had taken the trouble to let everyone know Elvis was coming, but it was still an amazing turn out for a singer who had not appeared in concert or recorded any fresh material for nearly two years.

Are You Lonesome Tonight?

As well as appearing with Frank Sinatra, Elvis recorded some classic songs including 'Are You Lonesome Tonight?' and 'It's Now or Never' in the spring of 1960. 'It's Now or Never' went on to sell nine million copies. The LP 'Elvis is Back' was also released and stayed in the *Billboard* chart for 56 weeks. The fans soon resumed their old habits, and Elvis was almost besieged wherever he went.

GI Blues:
a tremendous success

Although longer since he
left the Army, Elvis's hair
was never again worn in
the duck-tail style he had
before. *GI Blues* was
tremendously successful at
the box office, ranking 14th
in box office receipts.
Critics approved of his new
image – but Elvis worried
that the musical numbers
did not fit into the plot well
and the songs were not as
good as in some of his
previous films. Despite his
fears, the soundtrack album
stayed in the charts longer
than many of his others
and soon reached No.1.

Visited by royalty

While filming was in progress, a stream of important visitors came to see Elvis on set. In just one day he welcomed the King and Queen of Thailand, the wife and daughter of the Brazilian president, and three Scandinavian princesses (seen above) – not to mention Pat Boone, Minnie Pearl and Ernie Ford. The Colonel made sure that everyone knew that he was responsible for the royals – he was tirelessly dedicated to promoting anything that involved 'his boy'.

Opposite: A handsome and relaxed Elvis poses in his costume for *GI Blues*.

August 1960: Elvis gets serious in *Flaming Star*

In his next film, *Flaming Star*, Elvis plays Pacer Burton, the son of a
white settler and a Kiowa Indian woman, played by Dolores Del Rio. An
uprising by the Indians forces Pacer to chose sides – and the storyline
also covers the prejudice he encounters as a half-caste. With a respected
director, Don Siegal, and a cast of notable actors, *Flaming Star* was the
serious movie that Elvis had been wanting to make for some time.
Although a version with four songs was also shot, the final release only
had two – which greatly disappointed the fans.

The problems with prejudice that Pacer Burton experiences in *Flaming Star* were taken by some to be a veiled reference to the problems of African-Americans during their struggle for civil rights in the 1950s and 1960s.

Native American stuntmen taught Elvis how to handle his pistol correctly. The story was based on a popular novel by Clair Huffaker but had taken some years to bring to the screen.

Elvis takes a break

Above: Elvis protects Dolores Del Rio as the two of them escape from pursuers. Although *Flaming Star* was a critical success, it did not do as well at the box office as many of Elvis's other movies.

Left: Elvis with Barbara Eden, who played his romantic interest in *Flaming Star*. She later went on to star in the television series *I Dream of Jeannie*.

Opposite: Although Elvis made it through all the rough and tumble of filming without accident, he broke his finger while playing touch football between takes.

Christmas at Graceland 1960

Elvis pictured outside Graceland with his Rolls Royce, just before Christmas 1960.

Opposite top: Chief Wah-Nee-Ota inducts Elvis into the Los Angeles Indian Tribal Council in recognition of his role as a half-caste in *Flaming Star*.

Opposite bottom: Elvis with the Jordanaires recording a song for the soundtrack of one of his movies.

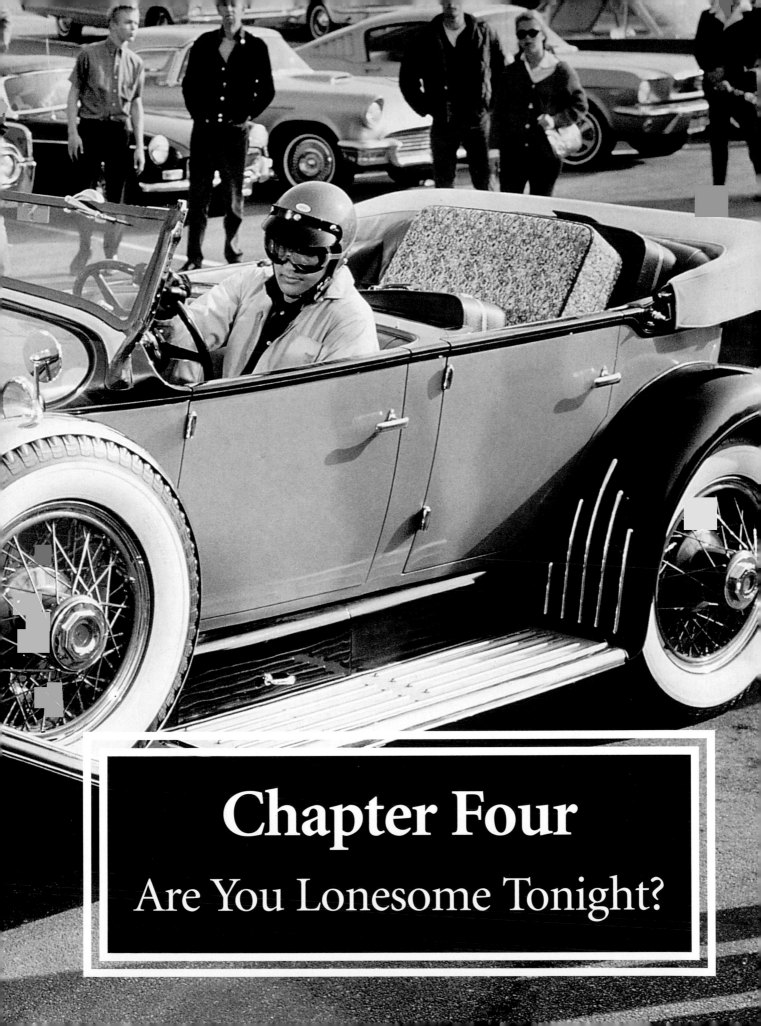

Chapter Four

Are You Lonesome Tonight?

A thoughtful Elvis strums his
guitar in a still from the 1961
movie, *Wild in the Country*.

During 1961 Elvis performed live only three times – two concerts at the Ellis Auditorium in Memphis and a charity event for the USS *Arizona* at Bloch Arena at Pearl Harbor, Hawaii. The live appearances had become a danger to all concerned – he had to arrive and leave in the greatest secrecy as the fans behaved so wildly in their attempts to reach him that there was a real risk that someone would soon get hurt. Elvis was also now concentrating on his film career, and since he went on to make three pictures a year for most of the rest of the 1960s there was little time left for concert tours.

The overall quality of Elvis's movies has sometimes been criticised, particularly since at the beginning of his film career several of his directors and fellow actors thought he was capable of even greater things. However, many of his movies were not only highly successful at the box office but were also well received by movie critics. In common with many other musical and comedy stars, almost all his movies were specifically written as a vehicle for their leading man – feel-good stories with lots of songs worked into the script. Elvis himself knew that he could also do darker and more complex roles, given the chance – he said several times in interviews that he wanted to become a serious actor and do dramatic parts. Some people blamed the Colonel for Elvis's failure to widen the range of roles he played, feeling that the desire to make ever more money made the Colonel short-sighted with regard to wider issues. His tireless negotiating for higher fees was certainly a factor in encouraging the studios to play safe and go for the tried and tested to protect their investment. *Flaming Star* and *Wild in the Country* had taken a different line and moved away from singing but they did less well at the box office. On the other hand, *Blue Hawaii*, a lightweight musical comedy built round an exotic location, was a massive hit. Several of the later films were therefore made to a similar formula, but unfortunately some of them suffered from short schedules and tight budgets. Elvis knew that they were not all that he wanted to do, that he had other ambitions to fulfil, but no one could deny that they were making money. Although he was offered some interesting and controversial roles, the Colonel turned them down, both because they did not fit the formula he had established and because they would not have been so lucrative.

Meanwhile, Elvis's personal life was as complicated as ever. At the beginning of the 1960s he was still dating Anita, but seeing other girls whenever she was not around – the Memphis Mafia were always there to cover for him. He had also remained in touch with Priscilla in Germany, and in March 1962 he began to talk to her parents about the possibility of her coming over to America. Understandably they were not sure about the idea, but he arranged for her to stay 'officially' with friends. Priscilla was still only 17, and Elvis himself was conscious of the potential problems if the press found out he was seeing such a young girl. Priscilla finally arrived in Los Angeles and after a few days they left to see Las Vegas, but all too soon she had to return. Despite all their precautions, Anita knew what was happening and decided it was time to move on.

Priscilla returned a few months later, to spend Christmas with Elvis at Graceland. Again the time seemed too short, so Elvis came up with the idea that she should stay in America and finish her schooling at a local Catholic school. Her parents refused to consider it at first, but eventually they gave in. Priscilla moved in with Dee and Vernon and was enrolled in the Immaculate Conception High School, but since Elvis was away in Hollywood working on yet another film, she soon moved into Graceland. When he was at home they did everything together and he began to mould her into his perfect woman,

change, but Elvis was delighted at the prospect of becoming a father. After Lisa Marie Presley was born on 1 February 1968, Elvis announced that he was the happiest man in the world.

Although his personal life seemed to have settled down, the problems in Elvis's career now came to a head. The fans were less devoted to seeing Elvis in every movie he made, and although a gospel album, *How Great Thou Art*, was selling steadily, his other records were not doing that well. The songs being supplied for film soundtracks were often so formulaic that even the Colonel was moved to protest. Unfortunately, much of the reason for that went back to the old arrangements he himself had set

up for writers requiring them to forgo part of their royalty before Elvis would record their song. Understandably, the best material was now no longer offered to him.

A change of direction was clearly needed and Elvis was ready to make it. The Colonel had arranged for him to appear in a TV special, which was to be broadcast just before Christmas 1968. It was to be recorded before a live audience – the first time Elvis had sung on stage for seven years. The Colonel wanted 'his boy' to sing a straightforward selection of Christmas songs, but NBC producer Bob Finkel convinced Elvis to go for a radical change of image. Director Steve Binder put together a show that

Stealing a kiss from Hope Lange, who played a psychiatric consultant in *Wild in the Country*.

Opposite: When Hope Lange's character falls in love with her client, it causes a scandal in the local community.

featured Elvis in black leather belting out his rock 'n' roll hits, and finished with a brand new song, 'If I Can Dream'. It was a total triumph. Everyone had forgotten what Elvis was capable of and hearing him sing the old hits with an exciting new freshness was a revelation to many.

Elvis himself was now determined to return to touring. From his new position of strength, the Colonel arranged a four-week booking at the brand-new International Hotel that was due to open in Las Vegas that July. It was certainly a gamble: Elvis's only previous appearance in Las Vegas had been a disaster; the room he was being expected to fill had a capacity almost twice those that current major headliners played; and it would all take place in a full glare of publicity. Meanwhile, some changes

had also been made in terms of how the records were recorded. The last few studio sessions in Nashville had been fairly disastrous, with only the minimum usable material laid down. Elvis was persuaded to try American, a small new studio in Memphis that had produced a string of hits under the direction of its principal owner, Chips Moman. The sessions were an unqualified success and Elvis recorded some of his best material to date, with the first single released, 'In the Ghetto', giving him a major hit and another gold record.

The opening night in Las Vegas on 31 July 1969, was the first time Elvis had performed a full concert in public for more than eight years. He was visibly nervous beforehand, but when he came out on stage and launched into his first number, his uninhibited

Elvis got on well with his three co-stars. Although there were originally no songs in the film, several were added after it was noted that the previous serious movie, *Flaming Star*, was not doing as well at the box office.

Opposite: In *Wild in the Country*, Elvis played Glenn Tyler, who serves time in a juvenile institution and then attempts to sort out his life. He is romantically involved with three women: Tuesday Weld's character tries to persuade him to stay with his own kind, Hope Lange's psychiatrist encourages him to go to college and Millie Perkins plays his childhood sweetheart.

love for the music combined with his instinctive sense of what the audience wanted created a sensational show. Those watching exploded with excitement and even the critics spoke of a mesmerising performance. By the end of the run his female fans were throwing underwear onto the stage, just like in the old days. The hotel management were quick to pick up their option on further shows, booking Elvis to appear twice a year for the next five years.

Unfortunately, while Elvis was now riding high in his career, his personal life was not going so well; although outwardly they appeared the perfect couple, Elvis and Priscilla were already having problems. After Lisa Marie was born, Elvis had made it plain to Priscilla that he was no longer physically attracted to her. Unhappy and unfulfilled, Priscilla had begun an affair with her dance instructor. No one dared tell Elvis – but it was only a matter of time before the marriage would begin to fall apart.

Fans cluster around a lei-clad Elvis as he stands in Los Angeles airport before flying to Hawaii to star in his next movie, *Blue Hawaii*. He was also scheduled to make several benefit appearances during his three-week stay on the island.

Can't Help Falling in Love

Elvis made several movies in Hawaii, including *Blue Hawaii* (1961), *Girls! Girls! Girls!* (1962) and *Paradise Hawaiian Style* (1965). 'Can't Help falling in Love', from the soundtrack of *Blue Hawaii*, was released as a single in October 1961 and went on to become a massive hit that year.

Behind bars again!

In *Blue Hawaii*, Elvis played Chad Gates, the son of a wealthy plantation owner. Pressured by his parents to give up his easy-going lifestyle to help run the family business, Chad disappears to the beach to play music with his native Hawaiian friends.

Opposite top: In a scene from the movie, Guy Lee as Ping Pong tries to spray water at Roland Winters as Fred Gates, Elvis, Angela Lansbury as Sarah Lee Gates and John Archer as Fred Kelman.

Opposite bottom: The soundtrack of *Blue Hawaii* featured 14 other numbers as well as 'Can't Help Falling in Love'. The music ranged across several musical styles. There were extensive shots of the Hawaiian scenery, with shooting at Waikiki Beach, Hanauma Bay and Ala Moana Park.

Dreading deep water…

Opposite: Angela Lansbury was cast as Elvis's mother – although she was only 35 at the time.

Joan Blackman with Elvis on the beach. During the filming of *Blue Hawaii*, Elvis revealed that he was apprehensive in deep water. Director Norman Taurog gave him the option of doing scenes on the beach instead, but Elvis bravely faced his fear and most of them were shot in or on the ocean, as originally called for in the script.

Follow That Dream!

Elvis and co-star Joanne Moore enjoy a little dalliance on the beach, in a scene from *Follow That Dream*. The title song from the film was released in April 1962 and went on to become a big hit.

Top: Elvis got lost on his way to the wedding of his secretary, Pat Boyd, to one of the Memphis Mafia, Bobby West, and so he missed the ceremony. He arrived just in time for the reception.

Opposite: Blue Hawaii was released not long before Christmas 1961, and quickly turned a profit. It grossed almost $5 million and the soundtrack album became the fastest-selling LP of that year.

Battered and bruised

In *Kid Galahad*, Elvis played a gallant boxer –
although the bruises are the work of the studio
make-up department. He was unhappy about
his appearance because his weight had recently
shot up, and he did not enjoy making the film.
One bright spot was taking boxing lessons
from former welterweight champion Mushy
Callahan, for whom Elvis felt deep respect. He
tried to impress co-star Charles Bronson, who
was playing his trainer in the movie, but the
veteran actor had little time for him.

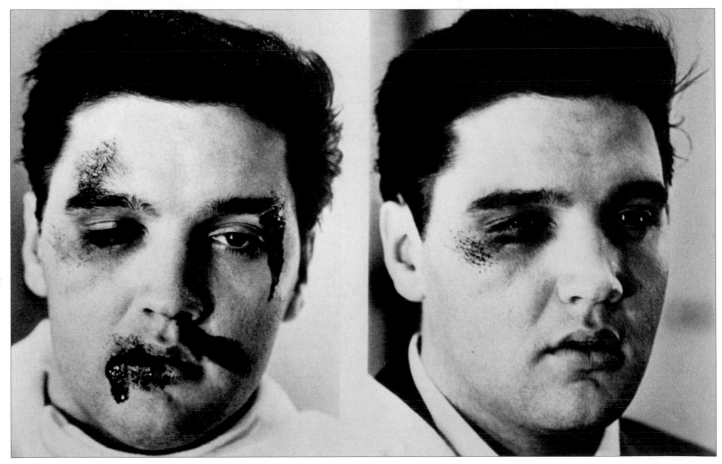

Elvis poses for stills during the filming of *Girls! Girls! Girls!*. Many well-respected musical and comedy stars have appeared in films tailored specifically round their talents – and Elvis was not the only popular music star to do so. Frankie Avalon, Herman's Hermits and The Beatles all made such films, which were marketed mainly to young audiences.

Summer of '62

Elvis and his entourage arrive in Seattle, accompanied by
police officers. They had come to the city for location filming
for *It Happened at the World's Fair* – the 1962 World's Fair was
being held there at the time.

Opposite: Elvis gets a manicure on Seattle's monorail. He and
the guys were prone to elaborate jokes to liven up the boredom
of filming. One of their favourites was to call for room service
after having removed all the furniture from the room – then to
have it all back in place by the time the manager arrived.

$9300 wardrobe

The storyline of *Fun in Acapulco* had Elvis as a former trapeze artist, who develops a phobia after his partner is severely injured. He gets a job as a lifeguard in a luxurious Mexican resort instead, and falls in love with the hotel's social director, played by Ursula Andress. Exteriors were shot on location in Mexico, but Elvis stayed on the Paramount lot in Hollywood. *Fun in Acapulco* went on to become the top-grossing film of 1963.

Opposite: Hitching a ride to the World's Fair. The Colonel always made sure there were plenty of photographers on set, and planted a story about Elvis's new wardrobe that had been supplied for the film. Hollywood couturier Sy Devore explained that the entire wardrobe cost $9300 – but did not include underwear as Elvis did not wear any.

1963: Viva Las Vegas

Ann-Margret and Elvis during filming of *Viva Las Vegas* for MGM in 1963. Ann-Margret was known as the 'female Elvis Presley' because of her sensual performing style, and rumours quickly began circulating that the two stars were having an affair. This time the rumours were true – despite the fact that Priscilla was already quietly living at Graceland.

Just Good Friends?

Even after their romance cooled, Elvis and Ann-Margret stayed close friends – right up to the end of his life – and he always sent flowers to her on opening nights.

Priscilla stays out of the public eye

Elvis enjoys a few nights off in Las Vegas. Priscilla was never seen with him in public during this period – everyone was afraid of what the press would make of the fact that he had such a young girl staying in his home, even though she was well-chaperoned.

Meeting Jim Brown

A group of Las Vegas showgirls are eager to chat to their celebrity guest.

Opposite: During a break in the filming of their respective movies, Jim Brown drops in on Elvis for a chat. Elvis had long been an admirer of the other actor's work and had wanted to meet him for some time. Elvis was currently filming *Roustabout*, in which he played a carnival hand with a knack for getting into trouble. Barbara Stanwyck was the boss and the two stars initially did not get on. Later they became friends and Elvis said the experience of working with her had inspired him to become a better actor.

Taking on the bad guys

Director Norman Taurog, on his fifth Presley film, was asked to try and bring *Tickle Me* in under budget – both to help Allied Artists and to ensure the film was completed. Since he was a fast and efficient worker, who got on well with Elvis, he managed to come in under what was already a tight costing.

Left: Enjoying a joke with one of his co-stars on the set of *Tickle Me*. Away from the cameras, Elvis had found a much more serious interest. He had recently met Larry Geller, a hairdresser who had introduced him to alternative religion.

Opposite: Elvis tackles the bad guy. *Tickle Me* saved Allied Artists from going under, its gross only coming in behind that of *55 Days in Peking* and *El Cid* in the company's history. It also made the usual profit for Elvis and the Colonel.

Cutting costs…

One way in which the Colonel maximised profits from *Tickle Me* was to arrange with Allied that the film soundtrack would only utilise songs already recorded by Elvis – which he guaranteed would not have appeared on a single or EP. In this way they could avoid the costs of recording original soundtrack material, while at the same time still being able to release a soundtrack record.

1965: Come into the desert…

Harum Scarum was a light-hearted film, set in the desert, produced by Sam Katzman and directed by Gene Nelson. The costumes were deliberately designed to make Elvis look like a modern Rudolf Valentino.

Above: While Elvis was making *Frankie and Johnnie* for United Artists, he was deeply absorbed by studies of religion, philosophy and the occult. Co-star Donna Douglas was both religious and spiritual, and Elvis spent hours with her discussing the books they had each read. He was rather overweight during filming, but his costumes were cleverly cut to hide it.

Paradise regained in 1965

In *Paradise, Hawaiian Style*, Elvis played Rick Richards, a helicopter pilot who operates a charter service. He had always enjoyed being in Hawaii before, but this time reporters noted that he seemed rather depressed. Nevertheless, he threw himself into the making of the movie, in which he sang some traditional Hawaiian folk songs.

Elvis had not had a song in the charts for a while, but now 'Crying in the Chapel', which had been recorded some time before and released in April 1965, was a top ten hit.

1967: Priscilla and Elvis say 'I do'

On 1 May 1967, Elvis and Priscilla Beaulieu are married by Nevada Supreme Court Justice David Zenoff, in a private ceremony held in a suite in the English-Tudor-style Aladdin Hotel in Las Vegas.

'It was about time' says Elvis

After the eight-minute ceremony was over, a press conference was held in the Aladdin Room of the hotel. Priscilla showed off her three-carat diamond ring and the happy couple kissed for the benefit of photographers. Reporters asked Elvis why he had finally decided to marry, and he replied, 'Well, I guess it was about time.' Priscilla's father told the newsmen that he had known from the beginning that the two of them would marry one day. Priscilla said later that they had both been so nervous before the ceremony that neither of them had slept the previous night.

Man and wife

The happy couple returned to Palm Springs after the reception, but three days later left for Memphis and on to the Circle G Ranch. Although most of the Memphis Mafia came with them, living on the ranch without the household staff gave Priscilla a chance to 'play house' and look after her new husband herself. At the end of the month, they held another wedding ceremony at Graceland – a less formal affair that included the entire Graceland staff and all Elvis's uncles, aunts and cousins, as well as his doctor, dentist, painter, horse trainer and electrician.

Nancy and Elvis

Despite all the rumours, after Lisa Marie was born it was Nancy Sinatra who held a baby shower for Priscilla.

When asked by a journalist what kind of part he played in *Speedway*, Elvis answered, 'I'm kinduva singin' millionaire-playboy-race driver, sir.' The journalist went on to ask if Elvis had ever played such a part before, and he replied, 'Only about 25 times, sir.'

Opposite: In 1967 Elvis filmed three movies: *Clambake*, *Speedway* and *Stay Away, Joe*, but this rate of work was not to continue for much longer.

Elvis's change of image

As well as Elvis and Priscilla, the party travelling to Honolulu included several members of the Memphis Mafia and their wives. They were also planning to attend a karate championship at the Honolulu International Centre, which was staged by Ed Parker, an old friend of Elvis. On his return from the holiday, Elvis was thinner than he had been for several years and had grown his sideburns longer.

Christmas 1968: Back to his roots

A leather-clad Elvis shows how it used to be, in the
Comeback Special aired on NBC at Christmas. The
Colonel had originally wanted him merely to sing a
few Christmas songs, but NBC producer Steve
Binder persuaded him to go back to his roots. He
challenged Elvis to walk down the street and see if he
was recognised by young people. Elvis was reluctant,
since he had not been out without an escort for some
years, but he decided to try. When no-one recognised
him, he agreed that his career needed a major boost
– which meant going against the Colonel's wishes.

Hit album follows Comeback Special

The *Comeback Special* featured live segments, pre-filmed concert sequences and casual jamming sessions, and loosely told the story of a young singer finding fame. The critics were ecstatic, praising both his performance and charisma. The show was the highest-rated programme that week, and the album that followed was also a hit.

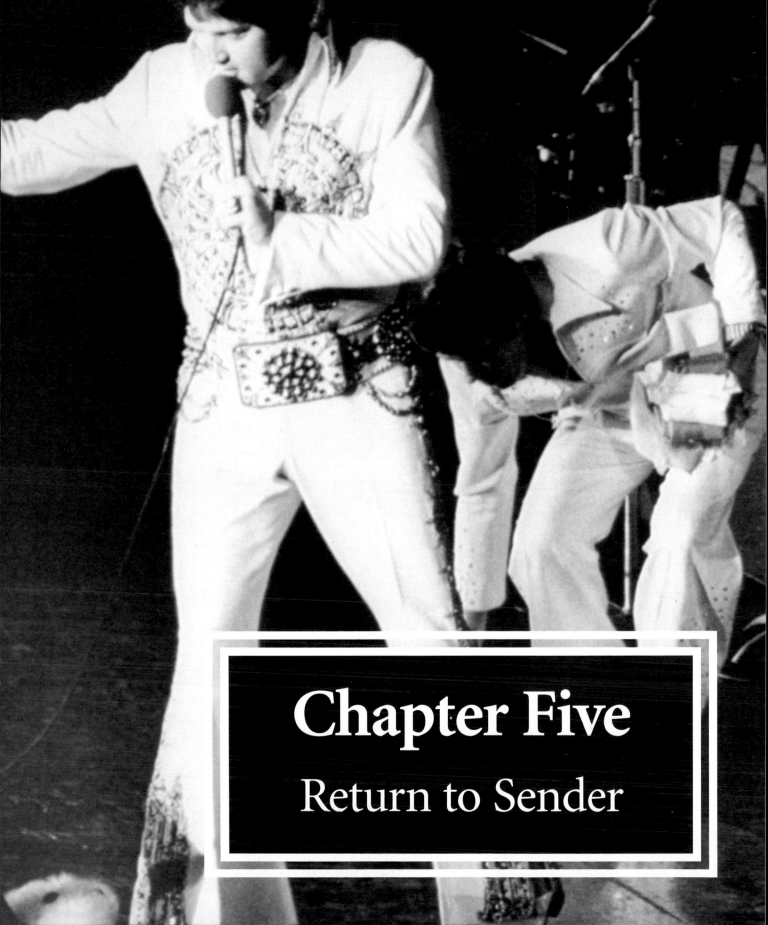

Chapter Five

Return to Sender

That's the way it is

The premiere of *Elvis: That's The Way It Is* was in November 1970. Elvis is seen playing a guitar during one of the scenes, and he is obviously not as fit, healthy and vibrantly alive as he had appeared in the *Comeback Special* just two years earlier.

The best man

Elvis was not only best man at the marriage of his old friend George Klein – he had also generously paid for the wedding and he hugged the blushing bride for the benefit of photographers. It was held in Las Vegas on 5 December 1970, and Elvis flew a dozen of his entourage in, also paying for them to stay at the International in his suite. Klein was a former DJ and member of the Memphis Mafia, and had appeared in small parts in several of Elvis's films.

Best of friends

Elvis, Priscilla and singer Glen Campbell. Glen Campbell had first worked as a session man for Elvis, but the two of them went on to become close friends.

Elvis and Glen

Elvis with Glen Campbell. Although he never smoked cigarettes, Elvis was very fond of cigarillos.

Opposite: One of the bridesmaids also gets a hug. The women very rarely got into the picture – although many of the Mafia were now married, their wives were very much in the background.

CASINO LOUNGE

THOSE SUPER TALENTED KOREAN DOLLS

THE **KIM SISTERS**

A JAPANESE DINING & COCKTAIL FANTASYLAND

BENIHANA VILLAGE

HIL

ELV

JACKIE KAHAN

JD SUMNER &

STAMPS QUAR

EXEC

BACCARAT AR

MU

PLUS DA G TO T FIASCOS BACCA

Star in the desert

When Elvis began appearing in Las Vegas regularly during
the 1970s, there was no doubt that he was a major star.
The Hilton Hotel chain had taken over the International in
June the previous year and before the deal was even signed
they were anxious to make sure that Vegas's premier
attraction would continue to appear in their hotel.

INSPIRATIONS

OE GUERCIO
CONDUCTING

E CLOCK

NITEBIRD   LOUNGE
THE BOSS OF THE BLUES
B.B. KING

VESTAL   VIRGIN
MORT SAHL
PLUS DANCING TO THE FIASCOS

LAS VEGAS HIL

Elvis on tour

Opposite: A shot from *That's The Way It Is*. Those involved in making the new documentary were deeply involved in their subject. They approached Elvis in concert as if he were a folk hero on a mythic journey. In addition, they had the latest mobile cameras and equipment, which brought movement and spontaneity to the filming.

As well as shots of Elvis performing, the filmmakers – Bob Abel and Pierre Adidge – included backstage material, shots of past glories and candid moments. The final film is one of the classic records of Elvis's career.

At the beginning, Abel had told Elvis, 'I want to shoot the real you… but you've got to be open with me. If I feel that you're posing or doing something, I'll just turn the camera off.' Elvis appreciated his honesty, and from then on was committed to the project.

Hard to live up to the image

At the press conference, Elvis was
accompanied by both the Colonel and
his father. A reporter asked Elvis if he
was happy with his image, but Elvis
pointed out that the image was one
thing, but a human being was another.
He then added, 'It's very hard to live
up to an image.'

Putting on the style in Vegas

The jumpsuits that Elvis wore in Las Vegas have become a symbol that represent this stage of his career. Most of them were designed by tailor Bill Belew, and they became increasingly elaborate. Sometimes they incorporated a cape – either waist or floor-length – and they were decorated with real gemstones and semi-precious jewels.

Elvis increasingly had a problem
controlling his weight. His poor diet
certainly didn't help, but the additional
weight was also due to lack of exercise.
He was taking a dangerous combination
of prescription drugs and he was
hospitalised several times. Many of
those close to him tried to cut his drug
intake, but Elvis was used to getting his
own way. Despite his bloated appearance
in some of the shows, the fans still loved
him and flocked to all his performances.

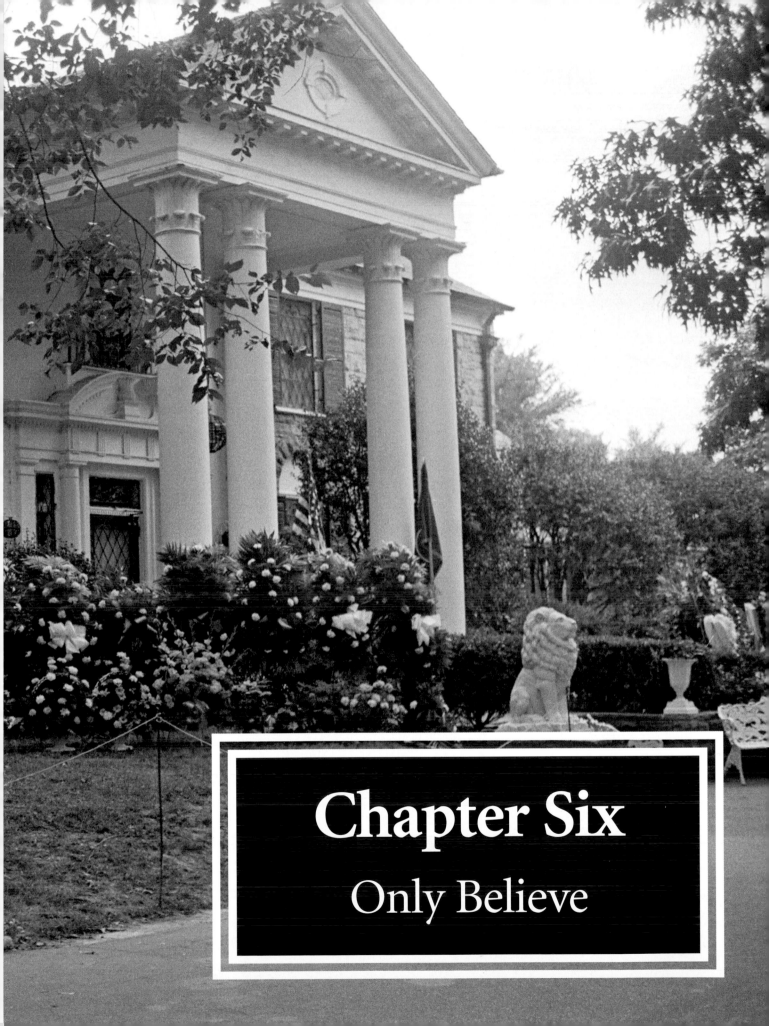

Chapter Six

Only Believe

Elvis has left the building…

Elvis's flower-covered casket is carried into the mausoleum at Forest Hill Cemetery. The pall-bearers included Memphis Mafia members Joe Esposito, Charlie Hodge and Lamar Fike, Dr Nichopoulos, and Elvis's cousin Billy Smith.

Opposite top: The hearse with its copper casket leaves Graceland, past saluting policemen. The funeral service had been held in the living room, with a sermon by Reverend Bradley of the Wooddale Church of Christ.

Opposite bottom: Local florists were flooded with over 3,000 orders for flowers and they covered the lawn in front of Graceland. It took four hours to move the flowers to the cemetery before the funeral.

Still a star…

The floral tributes from fans are often extremely elaborate and some are hand-crafted.

Inset: Elvis Presley's star on the Walk of Fame in Hollywood.

ELVIS PRESLEY

The original memorial from Gladys Presley's grave in Forest Hill Cemetery, with the Italian statue specially commissioned by Elvis and Vernon just after her death.

Opposite top: The name and image of Elvis lives on around the world.

Opposite bottom: Elvis's childhood home in Tupelo is now a tourist attraction – although it is furnished with home comforts the Presley's could never have afforded when they lived there.

The 1928 Kimball grand piano that Priscilla gave Elvis as an anniversary present, and which she had covered in 24-carat gold leaf both inside and out. It was first placed in the music room at Graceland but is now displayed at Nashville's Country Music Hall of Fame.

Opposite top: Elvis bought this pink Cadillac sedan for Gladys in 1956 – despite the fact she could not drive. It was the only Cadillac that he kept throughout his life and he promised it to Lisa Marie on her 18th birthday.

Opposite bottom: The living room at Graceland has been kept very much as Elvis left it and the décor and furnishings are flamboyant. The stained glass peacock was specially designed for the room – although displaying peacock feathers indoors is supposed to bring bad luck.

Bibliography

Elvis Presley: The King of Rock 'n' Roll, Robert Daily, New York: Franklin Watts, 1996

Elvis: Portrait of the King, Susan Doll, Illinois: Publications International Ltd, 1995

Last Train to Memphis, Peter Guralnik, London: Abacus, 1994

Careless Love, Peter Guralnik, London: Abacus, 1999

Elvis Aaron Presley: Revelations from the Memphis Mafia, Alana Nash (with Billy Smith, Marty Lacker and Lamar Fike), London: HarperCollins, 1995

The Ultimate Elvis, Patricia Jobe Pierce, New York: Simon & Schuster, 1994

Elvis's chart career looks like this:

- 149 songs in the *Billboard* Hot 100
- 18 songs made No. 1 in the *Billboard* Hot 100
- 9 albums made No. 1 in the *Billboard* Top 100 album chart.

IT'S THAT BIG S

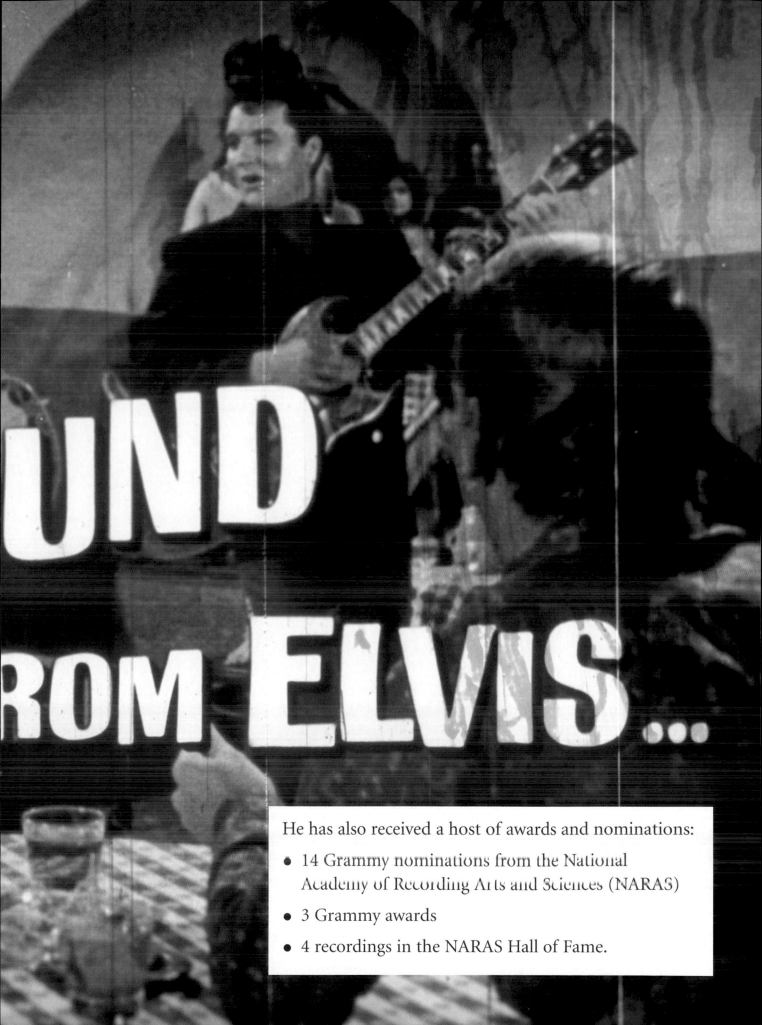

UND

ROM ELVIS ...

He has also received a host of awards and nominations:

- 14 Grammy nominations from the National Academy of Recording Arts and Sciences (NARAS)
- 3 Grammy awards
- 4 recordings in the NARAS Hall of Fame.

Elvis has also played a major role on-screen, with:

- 31 feature films as an actor

- 2 concert documentary films made during his lifetime

- 11 movie soundtrack albums, which made the top ten of the *Billboard* Top 100 album chart

- *Elvis: Aloha From Hawaii*, seen in 40 countries by 1–1.5 billion people and in more American homes than man's first steps on the moon.

Elvis played nearly 1,100 concerts between 1969 and 1977.

His charitable donations include the following:

- raised over $65,000 towards the building of the USS *Arizona* Memorial at Pearl Harbor with a benefit concert in Hawaii

- raised $75,000 for the Kui Lec Cancer Fund in Hawaii, from sales of audience tickets for rehearsals for the *Aloha From Hawaii* TV special

- for many years, Elvis gave $1,000 annually to each of 50 Memphis charities.

Elvis's home, Graceland, attracts over 600,000 visitors a year and is the most famous American home after the White House.

Elvis is the only person who is currently a member of three US Halls of Fame: Rock and Roll, Country and Gospel.

The first Elvis postage stamp had a print run of 500 million – three times the normal number for a commemorative stamp.

There are still over 625 active Elvis fanclubs worldwide.

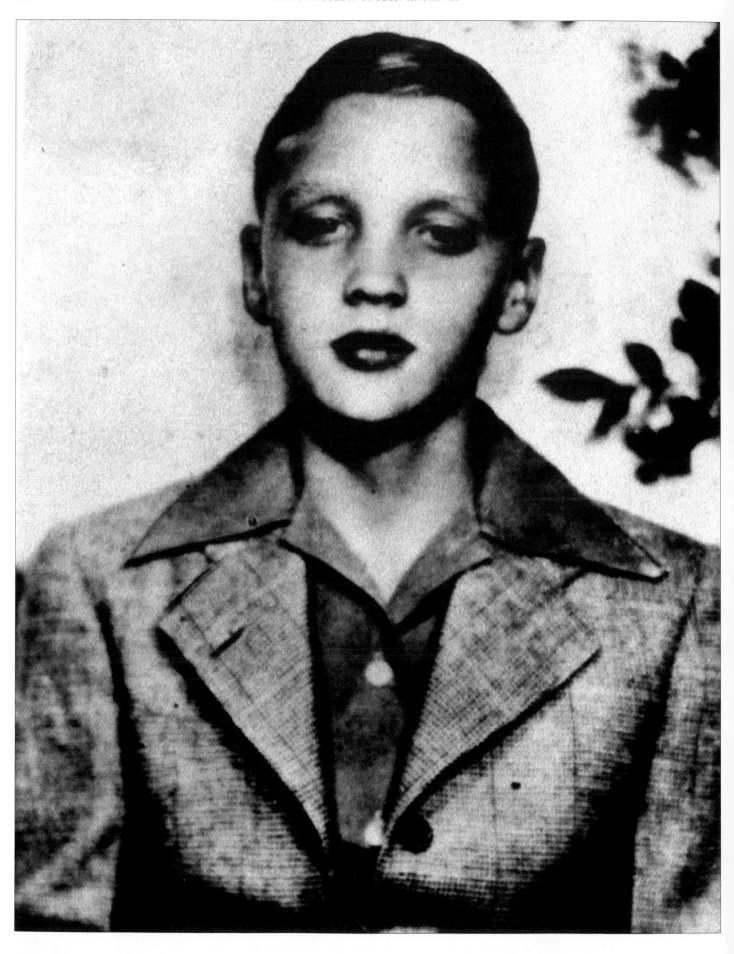

Chronology

1933 – 2002

1933

17 Jun Gladys Love Smith and Vernon Elvis Presley are married

1935

8 Jan Elvis Aaron Presley is born at his parents' home, 306 Old Saltillo Road; his twin brother, Jesse Garon Presley, is stillborn

1937

10 Nov Vernon Presley is found guilty of forging a cheque

1938

25 May Vernon Presley is sentenced to serve three years at Parchman penal plantation, a Mississippi state penitentiary, and Gladys and Elvis are left to live on welfare

1940

10 Oct Vernon is released from prison early because of good behaviour

1945

8 Jan Elvis receives his first guitar for his tenth birthday

3 Oct At the annual Mississippi–Alabama Fair and Dairy Show, held in Tupelo, Mississippi, Elvis sings 'Old Shep' in a live competition and wins second-place prize of $5 and free admission to the fairground rides

1948

Aug Governor Jimmie 'Pappy' Davis of Louisiana bestows the honorary title of 'Colonel' on his friend Tom Parker

12 Sept The Presleys move overnight to Memphis, after Vernon is caught trucking for a bootlegger and is fired from his job

1949

20 Sept The Presleys move into federal-funded accommodation in Memphis and life becomes more stable for nearly three years

1951

3 Jun Elvis starts work at Precision Tools

1 Jul Elvis is fired when it is learned that he is under-age

15 Aug   Elvis signs a contract giving Colonel Parker the right to manage his career, although he is still bound to Bob Neal for another year

'Mystery Train' enters the *Billboard* country chart, staying there for 30 weeks

8 Sept   Without Colonel Parker's knowledge, Elvis signs a new contract with the Louisiana Hayride for a further year from 8 November; his payment increases from $18 a night to $200

Oct   Atlantic Records bids $25,000 for Elvis to sign with them, but is turned down

10 Nov   At the annual DJ convention in Nashville, Elvis secures the recording rights to 'Heartbreak Hotel' from Mae Axton

13 Nov   The Country & Western Disc Jockey Association names Elvis Most Promising Country Artist

19 Nov   Colonel Parker, Elvis and Red West fly to New York City to meet Jean and Julian Aberbach of Hill & Range Music

20 Nov   Sun Records' contract with Elvis is bought for $25,000 by RCA Victor, while Hill & Range Music buys Sam Phillips's Hi-Lo music publishing company for $15,000

Nov   Elvis and Dixie Locke break up, as his new life keeps them apart too much

22 Nov   Elvis signs a contract making Colonel Parker his exclusive representative

1956

5 Jan Colonel Parker does a deal with Hill & Range Music, establishing a 50/50 partnership for five years with the newly created Presley Music Inc to publish the songs Elvis records

9 Jan Elvis rehearses 'Heartbreak Hotel', before recording it for RCA the following day along with 'I Got A Woman'; the next day, he records 'I Was The One' and 'I'm Counting On You'

15 Jan RCA gives Elvis a new convertible

17 Jan Release of 'Heartbreak Hotel'/'I Was The One'

28 Jan Elvis appears on Milton Berle's *Stage Show* on CBS TV. This was the first of several TV appearances including the Dorsey Brothers' *Stage Show* and Ella Fitzgerald's *Stage Show*.

30–31 Jan 'Blue Suede Shoes' is recorded during a two-day studio session

15 Feb 'I Forgot To Remember To Forget'/'Mystery Train' both reach No. 1 on the *Billboard* country chart, the first Elvis records to do so

22 Feb 'Heartbreak Hotel' enters the *Billboard* Top 100 at No. 68 and the Country's Best Sellers in Stores chart at No. 9

29 Feb 'I Was The One' enters the *Billboard* Top 100 at No. 84

1 Mar RCA is overwhelmed with 362,000 advance orders for the first LP, 'Elvis Presley'

3 Mar RCA's Top 25 Best Sellers list contains six records by Elvis

7 Mar 'Heartbreak Hotel' is No. 1 on the *Billboard* Country Best Sellers in Stores chart

13 Mar Release of the LP, 'Elvis Presley', which goes on to become the first in history to sell a million copies and stays in the *Billboard* extended-play album chart for a total of 68 weeks

15 Mar Colonel Parker becomes the sole official manager of Elvis

17 Mar Elvis appears on the St Patrick's Day *Stage Show* on CBS TV

28 Mar 'Blue Suede Shoes' enters the *Billboard* Top 100 chart at No. 88

1 Apr Elvis does a screen-test in Los Angeles for Hal Wallis of Paramount Pictures

Apr 'Heartbreak Hotel' is No. 1 on the *Billboard* pop chart and stays there for seven weeks; at the same time it is No. 1 on the country and western chart and No. 5 on the R&B chart

6 Apr Paramount Pictures signs Elvis to a seven-year, three-movie contract

May Release of 'I Want You, I Need You, I Love You', which stays in the *Billboard* Top 100 for 24 weeks and reaches No. 3, also getting to No. 10 on the R&B chart and No. 1 for one week on the country chart; the flipside was 'My Baby Left Me'

11 Apr *Variety* claims that 'Heartbreak Hotel' has become the first Presley record to sell a million copies

23 Apr Elvis begins a four-week engagement at the New Frontier Hotel, Las Vegas, but the audience does not respond well to him and he only stays for two weeks

Apr Elvis has talks with Liberace, who becomes a major influence on how he dresses and presents himself

Jun RCA releases the EP 'Elvis Presley', which goes on to stay in the *Billboard* Top 100 for 12 weeks, reaching No. 24

Jun *Time* nicknames Elvis 'The Pelvis'

1 Jul Elvis appears on *The Steve Allen Show*, singing 'Hound Dog' to a basset hound

20 Aug Elvis begins filming *Love Me Tender* in Hollywood for Twentieth Century Fox

3 Sept Although she does not drive, Elvis buys his mother Gladys a pink Cadillac

5 Sept 'Don't Be Cruel'/'Hound Dog' reaches No. 1 on the *Billboard* Top 100

9 Sept *The Ed Sullivan Show* gets the highest ratings in television history when Elvis appears

19 Sept 'Blue Moon' enters the *Billboard* Top 100 at No. 87

Sept In an interview in the *New York Daily News*, Elvis says there should be no draft, which encourages some young men to burn their draft cards

Sept	Release of 'Tryin' To Get To You'/'I Love You Because', 'Blue Suede Shoes'/'Tutti Frutti' and 'One-Sided Love Affair'/'Money Honey', none of which chart
25 Sept	Rumours circulate that Elvis is romancing actress Debra Paget, and that they will marry
26 Sept	Tupelo inaugurates Elvis Presley Day
30 Sept	Cardinal Spellman speaks out against Elvis, and Gladys is distraught to hear her son condemned
Oct	*Variety* names Elvis 'King of Rock 'n' Roll' and he also appears on the cover of *Rock and Roll* magazine
Oct	Elvis receives his draft questionnaire
3 Oct	'I Don't Care If The Sun Don't Shine' enters the *Billboard* Top 100 at No. 77
8 Oct	*Time* reveals that RCA has advance orders of one million for the single 'Love Me Tender' – an all-time high
10 Oct	'Love Me Tender'/'Any Way You Want Me' enters the *Billboard* Top 100 at No. 9
18 Oct	Elvis gets into a fight with a gas station owner, who asks him to leave the forecourt after his Cadillac draws a crowd of fans nearly causing a riot
19 Oct	The LP 'Elvis' is released
24 Oct	Elvis earns a gold record for 'Love Me Tender', his fifth of the year
27 Oct	The front page of *Billboard* announces that the Army plans to give Elvis a GI haircut, which causes fans to panic
31 Oct	Elvis starts to date Barbara Hearn
Nov	The EPs 'Elvis Vol 1' and 'Elvis Vol 2' are released
7 Nov	'Love Me' enters the *Billboard* Top 100 at No. 84, the LP 'Elvis' enters the Best Selling Packaged Records – Popular Albums at No. 7 and 'Love Me Tender' reaches No. 1 on the Top 100
14 Nov	At a Liberace concert in the Riviera Hotel, Las Vegas, Elvis is in the audience and after the show the two of them exchange jackets
15 Nov	The movie *Love Me Tender* opens in 500 theatres across the States and is a smash hit

21 Nov	Colonel Parker owns Elvis completely, after he gets Bob Neal to sign a contract to that effect, and pays off Hank Snow in lieu of a finder's fee
23 Nov	Louis Balint, an unemployed steelworker, is fined $19.60 for attacking Elvis because his wife's passion for the singer had broken up their marriage
28 Nov	The movie *Love Me Tender* enters *Variety*'s National Box Office Survey at No. 2
Dec	Release of the EP 'Love Me Tender'
15 Dec	Elvis appears at the Louisiana Hayride for the last time
Dec	'Heartbreak Hotel' is the *Billboard* No. 1 single for 1956

1957

4 Jan	Accompanied by Las Vegas dancer Dorothy Harmony, Elvis has his pre-induction Army physical at Kennedy Veterans Hospital
6 Jan	Elvis appears for the final time on *The Ed Sullivan Show*
Jan	The Army announces that Elvis is classed 1-A for draft
21 Jan	Start of the filming of *Loving You*, for Paramount
Jan	Release of 'Too Much'/'Playing For Keeps', which stays in the *Billboard* Top 100 for 17 weeks, at No. 2 for four of them
5 Mar	Gladys and Vernon Presley see Graceland and persuade Elvis that he should buy it
7 Mar	Elvis pays $102,500 for Graceland, far outbidding an offer of $35,000 from the YMCA
Mar	RCA gives Elvis a suit made of gold lamé, from Nudie's Rodeo Tailors in Hollywood which he wears for the first time at a concert in Kiel Auditorium, St Louis
10 Apr	'All Shook Up' reaches No. 1 on the *Billboard* Top 100 and stays there for eight weeks
13 May	Start of shooting on *Jailhouse Rock* for MGM, in Culver City
14 May	After swallowing the porcelain cap from one of his teeth, Elvis is rushed to the Cedars of Lebanon Hospital, California, with chest pains

June	'Teddy Bear'/'Loving You' is the first Elvis single to be distributed in the UK, and sells over a million copies	**25 Mar**	An Army haircut removes his famous ducktail hairstyle and sideburns
9 Jul	Premiere of *Loving You* at the Strand Theatre in Memphis	**28 Mar**	Elvis is sent to Fort Hood with his battalion for basic training
27 Jul	'Teddy Bear'/'Loving You' hits No. 1 on the *Billboard* Top 100 and stays there for 17 weeks, it is also at No. 1 for one week on both the R&B and the country charts	**1 May**	After the Colonel discovers that a soldier can live off-base if he has dependants in the area, Elvis moves his parents, along with his grandmother and Lamar Fike, into a rented house nearby and drives into base every day for duty
30 Aug	According to a report in *The Spokane Review* the following day, Elvis whips 12,000 fans into frenzy at a concert in the Memorial Stadium in Spokane, Washington; fans try to steal soil from the infield, because his feet have touched it	**June**	Since her health has been failing for some time, Gladys returns to Memphis for treatment
Sept	The single 'Jailhouse Rock'/'Treat Me Nice' is released in the UK and becomes the first Elvis record to enter the charts at No. 1 in England; it has already been released in the US and goes on to sell over three million copies in 12 months	**1 Jul**	*King Creole* is released to good reviews
		5 Aug	Gladys is taken into hospital and Elvis is granted compassionate leave to visit her
		11 Aug	Elvis receives his first RIAA Gold Disc Award for 'Hard-Headed Woman'
Sept	Scotty Moore and Bill Black leave Elvis because of their poor pay and lack of credit, although they play at some further recording sessions	**14 Aug**	Gladys dies of a heart attack in hospital
		16 Aug	Gladys's funeral is held in Memphis and she is buried at Forest Hill Cemetery
27 Sept	At Tupelo's Mississippi–Alabama Fair and Dairy Show, Elvis plays at a concert to benefit the Elvis Presley Youth Recreation Center, which he goes on to establish in his home town that December	**24 Aug**	As his unit is soon being sent to Germany, Elvis returns to basic training
		19 Sept	With his Army unit, Elvis travels from Fort Hood to Brooklyn, New York
28 Sept	The LP 'Elvis Presley' reaches No. 1 on the *Billboard* extended-play album chart and stays there for six weeks	**22 Sept**	Elvis and his unit leave on the USS *General Randall* for Bremerhaven, Germany, where they disembark to transfer to Friedberg
17 Oct	Premiere of *Jailhouse Rock* in Memphis	**10 Oct**	The entourage moves into a rented house, and Elvis moves off base to join them
8 Nov	*Jailhouse Rock* opens across the country and goes on to make a profit within three weeks	**23 Oct**	Bill Haley and the Comets play a concert in Frankfurt, which Elvis attends, posing afterwards in Haley's dressing room
19 Dec	Elvis receives his draft notice	**Nov**	Elvis goes on manoeuvres along the Czech border

1958

Jan	Release of 'I Beg Of You', which stays in the *Billboard* Top 100 for 12 weeks, reaching No. 12, and getting to No. 4 on the R&B chart and No. 2 on the country chart	**1 Nov**	Elvis is dubbed 'public enemy number one' by Russian leaders; actress Venetia Stevenson flies to Germany to see Elvis
		27 Nov	Elvis is promoted to private first class
5 Mar	Filming starts on *King Creole* for Paramount and later moves to New Orleans	**20 Dec**	After buying a used BMW 507 sports car from the company, Elvis agrees to pose for publicity shots
10 Mar	End of filming on *King Creole*	**Dec**	Elvis is named World's Outstanding Popular Singer, World's Outstanding Musical Personality and Favorite US Male Singer for 1958
24 Mar	Elvis is inducted into the Army and is sent to Fort Chaffee, Arkansas		

1959

Jan Robert Stephen Marquett, the son of an Army master sergeant, is pictured with Elvis and the photo becomes a 1959 March of Dimes poster

1 Jan Vernon crashes his son's black Mercedes into a tree, and in the confusion the German newspapers report that Elvis has been killed; Vernon is unhurt, but his passenger, a young secretary, is paralysed for a short period

8 Jan On his 24th birthday, Elvis is called by Dick Clark, who tells him he has been voted Best Singer of the Year, and that 'King Creole' is Best Song of the Year; that evening, Dick Clark's *American Bandstand* programme is dedicated to Elvis

3 Feb Elvis is deeply upset by the death of Buddy Holly, Ritchie Valens and Jiles Perry Richardson (the Big Bopper), along with their pilot, in a plane crash; all the musicians were friends

Apr A war memorial is erected in Steinfurth by Elvis and his Army unit

May In Friedberg, Elvis briefly dates Janie Wilbanks

1 Jun Elvis is promoted to specialist fourth class

3–9 Jun Elvis gets tonsillitis and is sent to Frankfurt Military Hospital

21 Jun Elvis and his entourage charter a plane and fly to Paris, where they stay at the Prince de Galles hotel on Avenue Georges V and frequent all the famous nightclubs

24–29 Oct Elvis gets tonsillitis again and is sent to the General Hospital in Frankfurt

Nov Priscilla Beaulieu is introduced to Elvis at a party

Nov Vernon meets Dee Stanley, an American in Germany with her husband and family

Nov After having karate lessons from Jurgen Seydel, Elvis has his photo taken in karate *gi* with a white belt

Dec The magazine *Elvis Monthly* is published in the UK by Albert Hand

25 Dec Elvis takes Priscilla to local festivities and meets her parents

1960

20 Jan Elvis is promoted to sergeant

Feb The magazine *Elvis Monthly* is released in the US

17 Feb The RIAA finally certifies the LP 'Elvis' a Gold Disc – although it has already sold more than three million copies

Mar A 'Letter from Elvis' is printed in *Photoplay* and he appears in Army fatigues on the cover

Mar *TV Radio Mirror* holds a contest to see who should be King of Rock 'n' Roll and Elvis is voted the winner

2 Mar Elvis leaves Germany from Wiesbaden airport and arrives the following day at McGuire Air Force Base at Fort Dix

3 Mar A photo of Elvis in uniform is featured on the front pages of newspapers across America; after being discharged, the ex-soldier tells the press there is no one special in his life and that he wants to concentrate on acting rather than singing. He then goes straight into the recording studio to produce some new songs

23 Mar Travelling by train to Miami, the railway track is lined with fans and photographers trying to get a glimpse of Elvis

3 Apr Release of the LP 'Elvis Is Back', which goes on to stay in the *Billboard* chart for 56 weeks, at No. 2 for three of them

3 Apr 'It's Now Or Never'/'A Mess Of Blues' is recorded, going on to enter the *Billboard* Hot 100 at No. 44 and climbing to No. 1 within five weeks; it remains in the chart for 20 weeks, also reaching No. 7 on the R&B chart, and becomes the *Billboard* Vocal Single of 1960; it carries on selling through the years, achieving sales of well over 23 million copies

4 Apr 'Are You Lonesome Tonight' is recorded and makes the largest chart leap so far, entering the *Billboard* Hot 100 at No. 35 but jumping to No. 2 within seven days; it stays in the chart for 16 weeks, also reaching No. 22 on the country chart, No. 3 on the R&B chart and staying at No. 1 in the English charts for four weeks

1 May Elvis and his entourage arrive at the Beverly Wilshire to begin filming on *GI Blues* for Paramount

12 May	*The Frank Sinatra – Timex Special*, featuring Elvis and recorded at the Fontainbleau Hotel in Miami Beach, is broadcast on 12 May on ABCTV, and also includes a host of other stars including Nancy Sinatra, Sammy Davis Jr and Peter Lawford
13 May	The change of style as featured on the Sinatra show upsets many fans; some critics accuse Elvis of deserting rock 'n' roll, or becoming lazy and no longer caring about the music, although others feel he has matured
Jun	*Movie Mirror* announces that 'The King of Rock 'n' Roll is Dead!' and reports that Elvis is now conservative
Jun	During a trip to Las Vegas, Elvis's entourage is christened the 'Memphis Mafia'; the name sticks
3 Jul	Vernon marries Dee Stanley, but Elvis refuses to attend the wedding
20 Jul	Vernon brings Dee and her three sons to Graceland, but they soon move out again to a house on Dolan Avenue
15 Aug	Filming begins on *Flaming Star* for Twentieth Century Fox
18 Aug	Preview of *GI Blues*, which becomes a big box-office draw despite being disliked by the critics
Sept	The Mexican government bans all Elvis films after a showing of *GI Blues* in Mexico City causes a riot
4 Oct	Filming finishes on *Flaming Star* and Elvis embarks on a short-lived affair with wardrobe assistant Nancy Sharp
30 Oct	'It's Now Or Never'/'A Mess Of Blues' goes in at No. 1 in the English charts, and stays there for eight weeks
11 Nov	Filming begins on *Wild in the Country* for Twentieth Century Fox
23 Nov	National release of *GI Blues*, which reaches No. 2 in *Variety*'s list of top-grossing films
23 Nov	A version of *Flaming Star* with only two songs is previewed in Westchester, California; it was later selected for general release and went into *Variety*'s list of top-grossing films at No. 12. A version of the film with four songs is previewed, but is later dropped
Dec	Elvis is inducted into the Los Angeles Indian Tribal Council by Chief Wah-Nee-Ota

1961

3 Jan	Elvis returns to Los Angeles to finish filming on *Wild in the Country*
8 Jan	On the set of *Wild in the Country*, Elvis celebrates his birthday with actress Hope Lange
18 Jan	Filming finishes on *Wild in the Country*
8 Mar	Governor Buford Ellington bestows the honorary title of 'Colonel' on Elvis
14 Mar	Elvis flies to California with his entourage to begin filming on *Blue Hawaii* for Paramount
24 Mar	Elvis flies to Hawaii
25 Mar	A benefit concert for the USS *Arizona* Memorial Fund, held at Bloch Arena in Pearl Harbor, Hawaii, raises $65,000
15 Jun	*Wild in the Country* is premiered, then released nationwide
1 Jul	The wedding of Red West and Patricia Boyd is attended by Elvis with Anita Wood
6–7 Jul	Elvis and his entourage travel by bus from Nashville to Florida
11 Jul	Filming begins on *Follow That Dream* for United Artists
Sept–Oct	Elvis spends some time in Hollywood, briefly flying to Nashville to record more songs
5–14 Nov	Elvis is coached for the boxing scenes in *Kid Galahad* by former junior welterweight champion Mush Callahan
Nov	Filming begins on *Kid Galahad* for United Artists
21 Nov	*Blue Hawaii* is released nationally and, by the end of the year, has grossed $4.7 million
30 Nov	Elvis is offered the lead in *Too Late Blues*, but the Colonel makes him turn it down

1962

8 Jan	Dick Clark dedicates the broadcast of *American Bandstand* to Elvis on his birthday
Feb	Colonel Parker persuades Elvis to turn down the part of Chance Wayne in *Sweet Bird of Youth*, the film of Tennessee William's play; the role goes to Paul Newman instead
7 Apr	Elvis flies to Hawaii to begin filming on *Girls! Girls! Girls!* for Paramount

11 Apr	Premiere of *Follow That Dream* in Ocala, Florida
15 May	The cast and crew return to Culver City to complete filming
23 May	National release of *Follow That Dream*, which did not do well at the box office
June	After protracted negotiations with her stepfather, Priscilla Beaulieu arrives in Los Angeles from Germany to spend some time with Elvis
27 Aug	Filming begins on *It Happened at the World's Fair* for MGM
29 Aug	National release of *Kid Galahad*, which goes on to gross $1.7 million by the end of the year
8 Sept	Elvis arrives in Seattle for further filming on *It Happened at the World's Fair*, staying at the New Washington Hotel
Oct	Release of 'Return To Sender'/'Where Do You Come From?', which reaches No. 2 on the *Billboard* Hot 100, No. 5 on the R&B chart and was No. 1 for three weeks in the UK
31 Oct	Premiere of *Girls! Girls! Girls!* in Honolulu
Nov	Elvis returns to Graceland for three weeks
21 Nov	National release of *Girls! Girls! Girls!*, which goes on to gross $2.6 million by the end of the year
Dec	Elvis is voted fifth top box-office draw by theatre owners and receives three Norwegian Silver Record Awards for 'Good Luck Charm'
Dec	Priscilla's parents are persuaded to let her come to America to spend Christmas with Elvis at Graceland

1963

Jan	Priscilla returns to Germany, but Elvis asks her stepfather if she can move to America and finish her education at a private school in Memphis
28 Jan	Filming begins on *Fun in Acapulco* for Paramount; although some shots were done in Acapulco, Elvis only filmed in Hollywood on Paramount's lots
5 Mar	Elvis is badly upset when his friend Patsy Cline, touring companion Lloyd 'Cowboy' Copas, and Harold 'Hawkshaw' Hawkins are killed in a plane crash
15 Mar	Filming is completed on *Fun in Acapulco*

Mar	Priscilla moves into Graceland with her parents' permission and is enrolled at the Immaculate Conception High School, an all-girl Catholic establishment
3 Apr	Premiere of *It Happened at the World's Fair* in Los Angeles
10 Apr	Nationwide opening of *It Happened at the World's Fair*, which went on to gross $2.25 million by the end of the year
29 May	Priscilla graduates from the Immaculate Conception High School
15 Jul	Filming begins on *Viva Las Vegas* for MGM; during the filming Elvis and his co-star Ann-Margret have an affair
5 Oct	Filming begins on *Kissin' Cousins* for MGM
21 Oct	Filming finishes on *Kissin' Cousins*
27 Nov	National release of *Fun in Acapulco*, which goes on to gross over $1.5 million by the end of the year
11 Dec	*Love Me Tender* is shown on television
Dec	Elvis is voted seventh top box-office draw by theatre owners

1964

1 Jan	Elvis is rejected in favour of George Hamilton to play Hank Williams in the film of his life, *Your Cheatin' Heart*, because Williams' widow feels the presence of Elvis would overshadow her husband's story
30 Jan	The yacht *Potomac*, which had once been owned by President Franklin D Roosevelt, is bought by Elvis
Feb	*Movie Life* runs an article about Elvis marrying Ann-Margret, but it refers to their screen wedding in *Viva Las Vegas*
7 Feb	The Beatles arrive in New York and Elvis sends them a congratulatory telegram
15 Feb	Elvis donates the yacht *Potomac* to St Jude's Children's Hospital
Feb–Mar	*Kissin' Cousins* has sneak previews in North Long Beach, California and Phoenix, Arizona
9 Mar	Filming begins on *Roustabout* for Paramount
11 Mar	An award for Americanism is given to Elvis by Shelby County and Memphis business leaders

Apr	*Kissin' Cousins* opens across the nation	**6 Oct**	Filming begins on *Tickle Me* for Allied Artists

Apr   *Kissin' Cousins* opens across the nation

Apr   First publication of the newspaper *The Elvis Echo*, edited by Paulette Sansone

20 Apr   Premiere of *Viva Las Vegas* in New York; filming finishes on *Roustabout*

30 Apr   Elvis and Larry Geller meet for the first time when Geller comes to cut Elvis's hair; Geller persuades Elvis to study the occult

17 Jun   National release of *Viva Las Vegas*, which goes on to gross over $4.5 million by the end of the year

22 Jun   Filming begins on *Girl Happy* for MGM

Jul   Elvis receives a South African Gold Record Award for 'Kiss Me Quick' on the MGM lot of *Girl Happy*

1 Aug   Johnny Burnette, a close friend of Elvis's, is drowned in California; Elvis is devastated

Aug   The UK press report that Ann-Margret and Elvis plan to marry, although she denies saying anything

6 Oct   Filming begins on *Tickle Me* for Allied Artists

11 Nov   National release of *Roustabout*, which goes on to gross $3 million by the end of the year

Dec   Elvis is voted sixth top box-office draw by theatre owners and is presented with an award as Tennessee's Entertainer of the Year

1965

8 Jan   Elvis celebrates his 30th birthday at Graceland

15 Mar   Filming begins on *Harum Scarum* for MGM

Apr   Elvis starts to visit the Self-Realization Fellowship Center and later meets its president, Sri Daya Mata

14 Apr   National release of *Girl Happy*, which goes on to gross $3.1 million by the end of the year, despite poor reviews

25 May   Filming begins on *Frankie and Johnny* for United Artists

28 May   Premiere of *Tickle Me* in Atlanta, Georgia

7 Aug   Filming begins on *Paradise, Hawaiian Style*

9–10 Aug	Elvis is absent without explanation from the set of *Paradise, Hawaiian Style*
27 Aug	The Beatles and Brian Epstein meet Elvis at his Bel Air home
21 Oct	Bill Black, one of the Blue Moon Boys, dies during surgery for a brain tumour
24 Nov	Premiere of *Harum Scarum* in Los Angeles
Dec	Elvis moves from Perugia Way, Bel Air, to Rocca Place in Stone Canyon

1966

20 Feb	Filming begins on *Spinout* for MGM
Feb	President Lyndon Baines Johnson visits Elvis on the set of *Spinout*
Mar	Felton Jarvis of RCA becomes producer of Elvis's recording sessions
31 Mar	Premiere of *Frankie and Johnny* in Baton Rouge, Louisiana
6 Apr	Filming finishes on *Spinout*
May	A short promotional film for *Paradise, Hawaiian Style* is released
Jun	Sneak previews of *Paradise, Hawaiian Style* in Memphis and New York City
11 Jun	Filming begins on *Double Trouble* for MGM
6 Jul	Nationwide release of *Paradise, Hawaiian Style*, which goes on to gross over $2.5 million by the end of the year
5 Sept	Filming finishes on *Double Trouble*
7–13 Sept	In an article, *Weekend* wonders if Elvis and Priscilla are secretly married
Sept	Elvis rents an ultra-modern house in Palm Springs as a private retreat
12 Sept	Filming begins on *Easy Come, Easy Go* for Paramount
13 Sept	A sneak preview of *Spinout* is attended by members of the Presley family, but not Elvis, who is still filming *Easy Come, Easy Go*
28 Oct	Filming finishes on *Easy Come, Easy Go*
1 Nov	The RIAA certifies the LP 'Elvis Presley' as a Platinum Disc after it has sold a million copies

23 Nov	Nationwide release of *Spinout*
Dec	Both her parents and the Colonel insist that it is time Elvis marries Priscilla or that she moves out of Graceland so, just before Christmas, he finally proposes
Dec	Elvis is voted tenth top box-office draw by theatre owners – it is the last time he appears in the poll

1967

9 Feb	Elvis buys the Circle G Ranch in Walls, Mississippi
Mar	Annette Day, co-star of *Double Trouble*, is given a white Mustang by Elvis
Mar	Filming begins on *Clambake* for United Artists in Los Angeles
10 Mar	After slipping in a bathroom, Elvis suffers mild concussion
22 Mar	National opening of *Easy Come, Easy Go*, which goes on to gross over $1.95 million by the end of the year
5 Apr	Nationwide release of *Double Trouble*, which soon grosses $1.6 million
1 May	Elvis marries Priscilla Beaulieu at the Aladdin Hotel, Las Vegas, in a private ceremony
2–6 May	Elvis and Priscilla honeymoon in Palm Springs, California, and then go on to the Circle G Ranch, accompanied by some of the Memphis Mafia
7 May	Elvis and Priscilla move to a new home in Hillcrest Road, Beverly Hills
29 May	A second wedding ceremony is held at Graceland, as many people were excluded from the first
Jun	*TV and Movie Guide* speculates that Nancy Sinatra might steal Elvis from Priscilla
12 Jun	Filming begins on *Speedway* for MGM, which also stars Nancy Sinatra
Jun	An article in *Screen Stories* suggests that Nancy Sinatra and Elvis are romantically involved
8 Sept	Filming finishes on *Speedway*
9 Sept	Elvis flies to Nashville, leaving Priscilla in Bel Air
18 Oct	Filming begins on *Stay Away, Joe* for MGM in Arizona

Nov	The cover of *Screen Life* features Elvis, and reports that he is to be a father	**Jul**	Filming begins on *Live a Little, Love a Little* for MGM in Los Angeles
22 Nov	Release of *Clambake*, which gets mixed reviews	**4 Jul**	Elvis donates his Rolls-Royce Phantom V to a charity auction; it raises $35,000
3 Dec	A special radio show, *Season's Greetings From Elvis*, is aired on RCA	**22 Jul**	Work commences on *Charro!* for National General in Arizona
8 Dec	TV premiere of *Tickle Me* on CBS TV's *Friday Night at the Movies*	**30 Sept**	The funeral of Dewey Phillips in Memphis, which Elvis attends
Dec	Elvis receives a Grammy Award for Best Sacred Performance for 'How Great Thou Art'; a pop poll names him No. 1 Male Singer and No. 1 Music Personality in America	**Oct**	Priscilla and Elvis are featured on the cover of *Screen Life*, with an article about them wanting another baby
31 Dec	The Manhattan Club in Memphis is hired by Elvis for a New Year's Eve party with 500 guests, but Elvis himself does not attend	**23 Oct**	Release of *Live a Little, Love a Little*
		28 Oct	Filming begins on *The Trouble with Girls* for MGM

1968

Jan	Elvis announces that he wants to do a singing tour of Europe, but the plan does not come to anything	**3 Dec**	The comeback TV special *Elvis* is broadcast on NBC TV and is the highest-rated programme that week
1 Feb	Lisa Marie Presley is born at the Baptist Memorial Hospital	**4 Dec**	The *New York Times* reports that Elvis has found his way home, and fans rush to buy his records again
Feb	Release of 'Elvis' Gold Records, Vol 4'	**31 Dec**	*Elvis* is shown in the UK on BBC2
7 Feb	Nick Adams, a close friend of Elvis's, commits suicide and Elvis is deeply affected		

1969

8 Feb	*Playboy* magazine honours Elvis in its feature on the year's music scene	**10 Mar**	Filming begins on *Change of Habit* for Universal and NBC in Los Angeles
5 Mar	Elvis flies to California for a recording session	**13 Mar**	National release of *Charro!*, which the fans love as Elvis looks handsome and rugged in a beard
8 Mar	National distribution of *Stay Away, Joe*	**Apr**	Gospel singer Clara Ward and Blues singer Mahalia Jackson visit Elvis on the set of *Change of Habit*
25 May	At a karate tournament in Honolulu, Elvis meets martial arts expert Mike Stone and suggests he teaches Priscilla	**2 May**	Filming of *Change of Habit* is completed
May	Priscilla buys a 1928 Kimball grand piano and has it gold-leafed inside and out; she gives it to Elvis on their first wedding anniversary	**May**	Elvis decides that he no longer wants to act in movies, but would like to return to singing
15 Jun	Elvis and Priscilla fly to Honolulu to see the USS *Arizona* Memorial	**21 May**	The Circle G Ranch is sold and the horses moved to Graceland
Jun	*TV Times* reports that Elvis fans no longer scream when he appears	**1 Jun**	Elvis goes on a diet to lose weight for his Las Vegas shows, before rehearsals begin in July
27–30 Jun	Elvis tapes a TV special for NBC TV, and is persuaded to appear in black leather and go back to his musical roots	**15 Jun**	'In the Ghetto' is certified gold by the RIAA
		31 Jul	At the International Hotel, Las Vegas, Elvis appears live in concert for the first time in eight years
		1 Aug	Elvis tells reporters that he plans a world tour, but it does not come off

2 Aug   A gold belt is awarded to Elvis at the International Hotel for 'the world's championship attendance record'

Aug   Fans travel from all over the world to see Elvis's Vegas shows

Aug   After a press conference, *Rolling Stone* reports that Elvis is 'supernatural', *Variety* calls him a 'superstar' and *Newsweek* compliments him on his staying power

Sept   'Suspicious Minds'/'You'll Think Of Me' is released and goes into the *Billboard* Top 100 for 15 weeks, reaching No. 1 in November for one week

22 Aug   The *Elvis* TV comeback special is broadcast again

3 Sept   National release of the film *The Trouble with Girls*

10 Nov   National release of the film *Change of Habit*

12 Dec   The LP 'From Memphis to Vegas/From Vegas to Memphis' is certified gold by the RIAA

1970

21 Jan   'Don't Cry Daddy' sells a million copies and is certified gold by the RIAA

26 Jan   A new season of concerts begins at the International Hotel, Las Vegas

23 Feb   Elvis's 57th and last concert of the run at Las Vegas

27 Feb   The first concert of a three-day booking at Houston Astrodome during the Houston Livestock Show, with Elvis performing two shows a night

1 Mar   Elvis flies back to Memphis to rest; after checking into the Baptist Memorial Hospital, he is informed that he has glaucoma in his left eye

1 Jun   Felton Jarvis leaves RCA to manage Elvis's recording career

10 Aug   The first concert in a new season at the International Hotel, Las Vegas

14 Aug   A paternity suit is filed against Elvis by Patricia Parker, a Hollywood waitress; her son Jason is born on 19 October 1970

26 Aug   Threats to kidnap or kill Elvis during a show are received; the FBI are called, but it turns out to be a hoax

7 Sept   The last concert of Elvis's current Las Vegas season

8 Sept   Nancy Sinatra opens at the International Hotel, Las Vegas; Elvis, Priscilla, Vernon and Dee are in the audience; Priscilla returns home after the concert, but Elvis flies to Arizona

9 Sept   Elvis gives a concert at the Veterans Memorial Coliseum in Phoenix, Arizona, and goes on to appear in St Louis, Detroit, Miami Beach, Tampa and Mobile over the next few days

Oct   Elvis becomes a special deputy in Memphis so he can legally carry a gun

Oct   Elvis has 14-carat gold necklaces made for all the members of the Memphis Mafia, inscribed with 'TCB' (standing for Taking Care of Business) and a lightning-bolt

Nov   Elvis tells the press that his marriage has difficulties

11 Nov   The premiere of *Elvis – That's The Way It Is*, a film of concerts and recording sessions, in Phoenix, Arizona; Portland, Oregon dubs this date Elvis Presley Day, when Elvis performs at the Memorial Coliseum. During the month Elvis also gave concerts at Englewood in New Jersey, Oakland, Seattle, San Francisco, Los Angeles, San Diego, Oklahoma City and Denver

1 Dec   Elvis meets Vice President Agnew

3 Dec   Elvis spends $20,000 on guns in a three-day shopping spree

5 Dec   Elvis attends George Klein's wedding in Las Vegas, for which he has paid

21 Dec   During a meeting with President Nixon, Elvis is given a Narcotics Bureau badge since he has offered to work undercover to help stamp out drug abuse and subversive elements in America

28 Dec   At Sonny West's and Judy Morgan's wedding in Memphis, Elvis is best man and Priscilla matron of honour

30 Dec   Elvis is taken on a tour of FBI headquarters in Washington DC

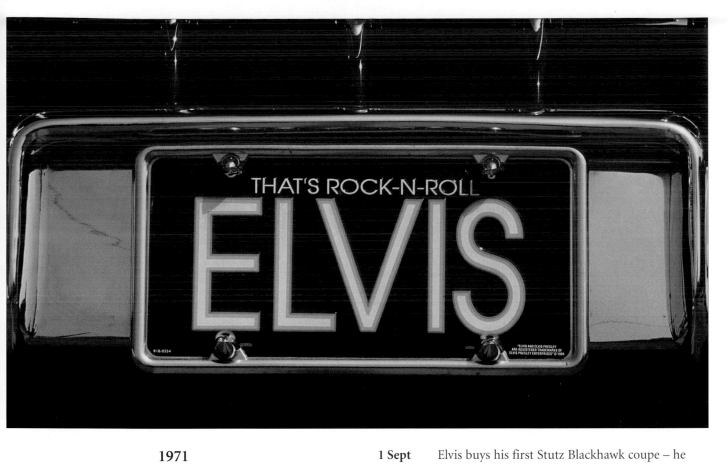

1971

9 Jan   Elvis is voted one of the Ten Outstanding Young Men of America by the Jaycees – members of the Junior Chamber of Commerce, a civic organisation for business and community leaders; it is to be the only award Elvis collects in person

Jan–Feb   A season of 57 concerts at the International Hotel, Las Vegas

27 Feb   Elvis flies to Memphis for seven days, then drives on to Nashville for a recording session

4 May   *Look* magazine features Elvis on its cover, with the first of a two-part account extracted from *Elvis: A Biography* by Jerry Hopkins

21 May   'Suspicious Minds' is named the Most Outstanding Single to be recorded in Memphis

1 Jun   The birthplace of Elvis in Tupelo is opened to the public

20 Jul   Elvis plays the first of 28 concerts at the Sahara Tahoe Hotel in Stateline, Nevada followed by another season of 57 shows at the Hilton Hotel in Las Vegas

Aug   Elvis and Priscilla move into a new house in Monovale, and Hillcrest is put up for sale

1 Sept   Elvis buys his first Stutz Blackhawk coupe – he eventually owns three

8 Sept   The Bing Crosby Award is given to Elvis by the National Academy of Recording Arts and Sciences

24 Oct   A 12-hour radio show, *The Elvis Presley Story*, is produced by Jerry Hopkins and Ron Jacobs

Nov   Elvis performs concerts in Minneapolis, Cleveland, Louisville, Philadelphia, Baltimore, Boston, Cincinnati, Houston, Dallas, Tuscaloosa, Kansas City and Salt Lake City

Nov   After Elvis passes a lie-detector test and a blood test, which prove he is not the father of Patricia Parker's son, she drops her paternity suit

30 Dec   Elvis tells his companions that Priscilla has left him

31 Dec   The *Elvis, 1971 Presley Album* is issued by *Screen Star*, with Elvis featured on every page

1972

26 Jan   The first of a new season of 57 concerts at the Las Vegas Hilton

Feb   Priscilla tells Elvis that she has been having an affair with Mike Stone

Apr	A series of concerts are played at Buffalo in New York, Detroit, Dayton, Knoxville, Hampton Roads in Virginia, Richmond, Roanoke, Indianapolis, Charlotte, Greensboro, Macon, Jacksonville, Little Rock, San Antonio and Albuquerque; many of them are filmed for the documentary *Elvis on Tour*
6 Jun	Elvis plays the opening concert of four at Madison Square Gardens in New York followed by concerts in Fort Wayne and Evansville in Indiana, Milwaukee, Chicago, Forth Worth, Wichita and Tulsa
6 Jul	Elvis meets Linda Thompson, a former beauty queen
26 Jul	Elvis and Priscilla are legally separated
4 Aug	The opening concert of 63 at the Las Vegas Hilton
18 Aug	Elvis files for divorce from Priscilla
4 Sept	Elvis appears in the last in the series of Las Vegas concerts and, at a press conference, the Colonel confirms details of an NBC television special to be broadcast the following January
Sept	Linda Thompson moves into Graceland
20 Oct	Television premiere of *Change of Habit* on NBC's *Friday Night at the Movies*
1 Nov	Release of *Elvis on Tour*, which grosses nearly half a million dollars in one week
Nov	A series of concerts are played in Lubbock, Tucson, El Paso, Oakland, San Bernadino, Long Beach and Honolulu
Dec	A Grammy for Best Inspirational Performance is awarded for the LP 'He Touched Me'; *Elvis on Tour* is voted Best Documentary of 1972 by the Hollywood Foreign Press Association and nominated for a Golden Globe Award

1973

9 Jan	Elvis arrives in Honolulu to begin rehearsals for *Elvis: Aloha From Hawaii*
14 Jan	*Elvis: Aloha From Hawaii* is broadcast to 40 countries worldwide
15 Jan	A second broadcast of *Elvis: Aloha From Hawaii* is seen in 28 European countries
18 Jan	Elvis and his entourage fly to Las Vegas and rehearsals begin for the opening of a season in Las Vegas

26 Jan	Elvis performs the opening concert of 54 at the Las Vegas Hilton
Jan	Elvis gives Muhammad Ali a flamboyant, jewel-encrusted robe with 'People's Champion' inscribed across the back; Ali wears it before his 14 February fight against Joe Bugner in Las Vegas
Feb	Due to the interaction of the cocktail of drugs he is now taking, Elvis misses several concerts in Las Vegas and is treated by a succession of doctors
18 Feb	At Elvis's midnight show, four men rush on to the stage, apparently to attack Elvis, who knocks one back into the audience; the others are removed by security, but they turn out to be over-excited fans
23 Feb	Elvis finishes the final concert in Las Vegas, but stays on to see Ann-Margret opening and several other shows
9 Mar	Returning to Graceland, Elvis recuperates with Linda Thompson and the Memphis Mafia
2 Apr	Elvis persuades Ed Parker to award him a sixth-degree black belt in *kenpo* karate
4 Apr	*Elvis: Aloha From Hawaii* is expanded and broadcast as a TV special across the US on NBC TV
Apr	Elvis persuades Kang Rhee to award him a seventh-degree black belt in *Pasaryu* karate
Apr	Concerts are played in Phoenix, Anaheim, Fresno, San Diego, Portland, Spokane, Seattle and Denver
4 May	Elvis is due to play 25 concerts at the Sahara Tahoe Hotel in Stateline, Nevada, but several concerts are cancelled due to illness, as years of prescription drug abuse begin to take their toll
13 May	After a special Mother's Day concert, Elvis donates money to the Barton Memorial Hospital in memory of his mother
18 May	Ill and exhausted, Elvis returns to Memphis
May	A private investigator, John O'Grady, is hired to investigate where Elvis is getting his prescription drugs
Jun	Concerts are played in Mobile, Atlanta, Uniondale, Nassau, Pittsburgh, Cincinnati, St Louis, Nashville and Oklahoma City. After returning to Memphis in July, Elvis begins a series of recording sessions

6 Aug	The first concert in a planned series of 59 at the Las Vegas Hilton, although Elvis misses two due to illness
Aug	After a major argument the partnership of Colonel Parker and Elvis breaks up, but is soon re-instated
9 Oct	The divorce of Elvis and Priscilla is finalised in Santa Monica
Oct	Elvis is hospitalised for two weeks after an extreme drug reaction and is put through a drug withdrawal programme
Nov	*Movie World* features Elvis and Priscilla on its cover and reports that Elvis has collapsed after the divorce
10–16 Dec	Elvis records several songs in a session at Stax Studios in Memphis, but using a mobile recording unit provided by RCA

1974

Jan	Colonel Parker and Elvis form Boxcar Enterprises to handle the merchandising of Elvis-related products not connected to movies or records; Boxcar Records is also created
26 Jan	The first concert in a series of 29 at the Las Vegas Hilton ending 9 February
Mar	*Silver Screen* features Elvis on its cover and an article speculates that he will marry Linda Thompson
Mar	Concerts are played in Tulsa, Houston, Monroe in Louisiana, Auburn in Alabama, Montgomery, Charlotte, Roanoke, Hampton Roads, Richmond, Greensboro, Murfreesboro in Tennessee, Knoxville and Memphis
Mar	Dr George Nichopoulos (Dr Nick) attends Elvis full time during the tour so he can monitor his drug intake
May	Concerts are played in San Bernadino, Los Angeles and Fresno followed by 22 concerts at the Sahara Tahoe Hotel in Stateline, Nevada
Jun	During a 21-day tour, concerts are played in Fort Worth, Baton Rouge, Amarillo, Des Moines, Cleveland, Providence, Philadelphia, Niagara Falls, Columbus, Louisville, Bloomington, Milwaukee, Kansas City, Omaha and Salt Lake City

19 Aug	The first concert in a planned series of 29 at the Las Vegas Hilton; Elvis is ill and has to cancel two performances
Aug	Linda Thompson is replaced by Sheila Ryan as Elvis's official girlfriend
19 Sept	Linda Thompson appears back on the scene
29 Sept	Local papers are enthusiastic after Elvis performs at a concert at the Olympian Stadium in Detroit
Oct	Concerts are played in St Paul in Minnesota, Dayton, Indianapolis, Wichita, San Antonio and Abilene followed by eight concerts at the Sahara Tahoe Hotel in Stateline, Nevada
Nov	*Rolling Stone* reports that Elvis is still a superstar and he wins a Grammy for Best Inspirational Performance for 'How Great Thou Art', which is featured on the LP 'Elvis Recorded Live'
Dec	Elvis recuperates from a strenuous year at Graceland and an article in *Celebrity* comments on his poor health

1975

29 Jan	Elvis is rushed to hospital at midnight with severe stomach pains, and is admitted to get his drug use back under control
5 Feb	Elvis's father Vernon has a heart attack and is admitted to the same hospital
10–13 Mar	Elvis records at RCA's Hollywood studios
18 Mar	The first of a scheduled 29 shows at the Las Vegas Hilton
28 Mar	Barbra Streisand talks to Elvis about taking the co-starring role in the remake of *A Star is Born*, but the Colonel handles negotiations and the project founders
Apr	Elvis buys a 96-passenger Convair 880 plane, which he redecorates in blue and white, and christens the 'Lisa Marie'. It is delivered on 10 November
Apr–Jul	Concerts are played in Macon, Jacksonville, Tampa, Lakeland, Murfreesboro, Atlanta, Monroe, Lake Charles in Louisiana, Huntsville in Alabama, Mobile, Houston, Dallas, Shreveport, Jackson, Memphis, Oklahoma City, Terre Haute in Indiana, Cleveland, Charleston, Niagara Falls, Springfield, New Haven, Uniondale, Norfolk and Greensboro

5 May	Elvis plays a benefit concert at the State Fair Coliseum in Jackson, Mississippi, and raises $108,000 for hurricane survivors in McComb, Mississippi
Jul	Elvis has cosmetic surgery to give his eyes a more youthful look
23–24 Jul	During a show at Asheville, North Carolina, Elvis gives away a $6,500 ring to a fan in the audience
27 Jul	After buying 14 Cadillac Eldorados, Elvis gives them all away
Aug	Priscilla and Mike Stone split up; Priscilla begins her acting career; Elvis is still in poor health and is putting on weight
18 Aug	Although he is due to perform a series of concerts at the Las Vegas Hilton, most of them are cancelled due to Elvis's poor health
21 Aug	Elvis is admitted to hospital for two weeks and attempts are made to sort out some of his medical problems
Aug	Linda Thompson leaves to pursue an acting career, and Elvis briefly begins seeing Jo Cathy Brownlee
10 Nov	The 'Lisa Marie' is finally delivered
28 Nov	Elvis flies to Las Vegas to rehearse for 17 shows at the Las Vegas Hilton, and Linda Thompson returns briefly to support him
31 Dec	A New Year's Eve concert in Pontiac, Michigan, breaks concert receipt records

1976

Jan	Elvis buys five cars and gives them away
22 Jan	A new agreement giving the Colonel 50/50 partnership on live dates comes into effect
Feb	*Movie Stars* features Elvis and Linda Thompson, with an article speculating that they will marry – in fact they are already well on the way to splitting up
2–8 Feb	Elvis records at Graceland, using temporary equipment installed by RCA
20 Apr	Elvis invests in Presley Center Courts, Inc, which plans to run racquet-ball clubs; he is a 25 per cent partner, along with his physician, Dr George Nichopoulos, Joe Esposito and real estate developer Michael McMahon; Elvis pulls out when the venture is proved to be losing money
Apr–Jun	Concerts are played in Kansas City, Omaha, Denver, San Diego, Long Beach, Seattle, 15 shows at the Sahara Tahoe Hotel in Stateline, Nevada, Bloomington, Ames in Iowa, Oklahoma City, Odessa in Texas, Lubbock, Tucson, El Paso, Fort Worth, Atlanta, Omaha, Buffalo, Rhode Island, Largo in Maryland, Philadelphia, Richmond and Greensboro
13 Jul	Vernon fires Red and Sonny West, along with Dave Hebler
Jul–Aug	Concerts are performed at Shreveport, Baton Rouge, Fort Worth, Tulsa, Memphis, Louisville, Charleston, Syracuse, Rochester, Hartford, Springfield, New Haven, Hampton Roads, Roanoke, San Antonio, Houston, Mobile, Tuscaloosa and Macon
Sept–Oct	Elvis performs concerts in Jacksonville, Florida, Alabama, Arkansas, Duluth, Minneapolis, Sioux Falls, Madison, South Bend, Kalamazoo, Champaign, Cleveland, Evansville, Fort Wayne, Dayton and Carbondale, Illinois
29 Oct	Another recording session is arranged at Graceland, but Elvis is not well enough to do much work
19 Nov	Elvis meets Ginger Alden, a former beauty queen
Nov	Billy Carter, the President's brother, comments that Elvis is guarded better than the president after he and his wife visit Graceland
Nov	Elvis performs a series of concerts in Nevada, Oregon and California, and Ginger Alden is invited to join him; Linda Thompson finally leaves for good
2 Dec	A new season of 15 concerts begins at the Las Vegas Hilton; the last is on 12 December and this time Elvis does not miss any performances
Dec	Elvis gives Ginger a Lincoln Mark V
9 Dec	Vernon is admitted to hospital with a suspected heart attack
27 Dec	The first of five concerts is performed in Wichita, Kansas; the others are in Texas, Alabama, Georgia and Pennsylvania

1977

Jan   Priscilla and Elvis are featured on the cover of *TV Star Parade*, with an article speculating that they have secretly remarried

Jan   Elvis spends his birthday with Ginger and her sister Rosemary in Palm Springs

20 Jan   A recording session is scheduled in Nashville, but Elvis cancels due to a sore throat

26 Jan   Elvis proposes to Ginger and gives her a diamond ring

1 Feb   Elvis and Ginger celebrate Lisa's ninth birthday with her in Los Angeles

Feb–Mar   A series of 17 concerts are played in Florida, Alabama, Georgia, South Carolina, Tennessee, North Carolina, Arizona, Texas, Oklahoma and Louisiana

3 Mar   Elvis takes Ginger and her family on a two-week vacation to Hawaii

Apr   A series of concerts is booked through North Carolina, Michigan, Ohio, Wisconsin, Minnesota and Illinois, but Elvis collapses during the tour, and is taken back to Memphis and admitted to the Baptist Memorial Hospital

5 Apr   Elvis leaves hospital and spends some time recuperating at Graceland

Apr   Elvis argues with Ginger and invites Alicia Kerwin to accompany him on a trip to Las Vegas and Palm Springs

May–Jun   A series of 23 concerts is performed across 18 states with only 16 days' rest during the punishing schedule; Ginger accompanies Elvis for most of the time

May   Newspapers report that the Colonel is planning to sell Elvis's contract to pay off his gambling debts

1 Jun   The Colonel announces details of a forthcoming CBS concert special, to be filmed on the next tour

18 Jun   *Photoplay* awards Elvis Gold Medal Awards for Favorite Variety Star and Favorite Rock Music Star

27 Jun   Elvis returns to Graceland to recuperate

Jul   Release of 'Way Down'/'Pledging My Love', which goes into the *Billboard* country chart for 17 weeks, reaching No. 1 in August; it also spends 21 weeks in the Top 100 chart, reaching No. 18, and reaches No. 14 on the easy listening chart; in the UK it becomes Elvis's 17th No. 1 record

Jul   The book, *Elvis: What Happened?*, is published, written by Steve Dunleavy and based on material from the three ex-members of the Memphis Mafia: Red West, Sonny West and Dave Hebler

Jul–Aug   Lisa Marie arrives at Graceland for a two-week visit; Elvis rents the Libertyland amusement park for several hours after closing time as a present for Lisa Marie and her friends

16 Aug   Elvis is found dead in his bathroom at Graceland by Ginger Alden; the cause of death is announced as a heart attack, but the later autopsy rules that he died from a drug overdose

17 Aug   With his body lying in state at Graceland, thousands of fans congregate outside, waiting to file past the coffin and get one last glimpse of Elvis

18 Aug   Elvis's funeral is held at Graceland, and he is laid to rest next to his mother at Forest Hill Cemetery

23 Aug   The Colonel convinces Vernon to sign a contract giving all rights to the marketing of Elvis-related products to Boxcar Enterprises; 50 per cent of income is to be distributed equally between the Colonel and the Elvis Presley estate, with the remaining 50 per cent for expenses and salaries; anything left after expenses is to be divided 56 per cent to the Colonel and the rest between the estate and Tom Diskin

21 Aug   RCA reports that it has sold over eight million Elvis records in the six days since his death

29 Aug   Three men attempt to steal Elvis's body; charges are later dropped when the court believes they were trying to prove the coffin was empty and that Elvis is still alive

7 Sept   A shorter version of the documentary *Elvis on Tour* is shown on NBC TV to top ratings

12 Sept   'Way Down' is certified gold by the RIAA

3 Oct   CBS TV shows *Elvis in Concert*, a one-hour special that was filmed during his last tour

27 Oct	The bodies of Elvis and his mother are removed from Forest Hill Cemetery and re-interred at Graceland in the Meditation Garden
Nov	Elvis's physician, Doctor Nichopoulos suspended while the court investigates his prescription of drugs to Elvis
Nov	A Broadway show, *Elvis Lives*, wins the *New York Evening Standard* award for Best Musical of the Year
20 Nov	A three-hour television special, *Memories of Elvis*, is broadcast on NBC TV

1978

Jan	Elvis has left his entire estate to Lisa Marie, but Priscilla and the other trustees are horrified to discover there is no money left
1 Feb	*Playboy* inducts Elvis into its Music Hall of Fame
16–18 Aug	On the first anniversary of Elvis's death, thousands of fans gather outside Graceland
1–10 Sept	An Elvis Presley Convention is held at the Las Vegas Hilton – it becomes an annual event
8 Sept	A bronze statue of Elvis is unveiled in the lobby of the Las Vegas Hilton

1979

Jan	Investigations into Elvis's finances reveal he was not a member of Broadcast Music Inc, and so has probably lost millions of dollars in royalty payments
8 Jan	The anniversary of Elvis's birth is celebrated in Memphis and Tupelo, and becomes an annual event
11 Feb	ABC TV broadcasts *Elvis*, the story of his life with Kurt Russell playing Elvis and Shelley Winters as Gladys
Apr	A newsletter about Elvis, called *Reflections*, is started by two ex-members of the Memphis Mafia
May	Two tons of grey marble from Elvis's first tomb at the Forest Hill Cemetery are bought by Bill Carwile; he cuts it up into 44,000 small pieces, which he sells for $80 each
26 Jun	Vernon dies of heart failure, and is later buried next to Elvis and Gladys
17 Aug	An Elvis Presley Chapel is dedicated in Elvis Presley Park in Tupelo

1980

8 Feb NBC TV broadcasts *Elvis Remembered: Nashville to Hollywood*, which is a shortened version of *Nashville Remembers Elvis on His Birthday*

8 May Minnie Mae Presley, Elvis's grandmother, dies in Memphis

24 Jun Singer Margot Heine Kuzma alleges in the German *Globe* that her son Leroy is the son of Elvis

1981

The IRS claims that Elvis's estate owes $14.6 million in inheritance taxes, plus a further $2.3 million in tax interest; to raise funds and protect her daughter's inheritance, Priscilla plans to open Graceland to the public

3 Apr Premiere in Memphis of a documentary, *This is Elvis*, made by Warner Brothers

Jul The courts decide that Boxcar Enterprises has no right to distribute Elvis-related merchandise

Jul–Aug At the Las Vegas Hilton, *Elvis, An American Musical* is performed

1982

7 Jun The downstairs rooms at Graceland are opened to the public

Oct Release of 'The Elvis Medley', which goes on to stay in the *Billboard* Top LPs chart for nine weeks

1983

8 Jan An Elvis Presley Museum is opened in London

1984

Aug *Life* runs an article pointing out that the Elvis Presley industry is earning ten times as much as he did when he was alive

Aug–Nov The interior of Graceland is filmed for a video, *Elvis Presley's Graceland*; Elvis is posthumously awarded the WC Handy Award from the Blues Foundation for 'keeping the blues alive'; Elvis is also posthumously awarded the first Golden Hat Award from the Academy of Country Music for his influence on country music

1985

5 Jan A TV special, *Elvis: One Night With You* – a complete record of one of the performances taped for the NBC TV *Elvis* comeback special – is shown on Home Box Office cable TV and repeated throughout the month

Aug A syndicated TV special, *Elvis: The Echo Will Never Die*, features people who knew or worked with Elvis

1986

Feb Elvis is, posthumously, one of the first to be inducted into the Rock and Roll Hall of Fame in Cleveland, Ohio

1987

Aug On a phone-in run by *USA Today*, fans vote 'Suspicious Minds' their No. 1 favourite Elvis song, with 'Love Me Tender' No. 2

Elvis is posthumously granted an Award of Merit at the American Music Awards

1988

The 1956 recording of 'Hound Dog' is inducted into the NARAS Hall of Fame

7–8 Feb A mini-series, *Elvis and Me*, based on Priscilla's book about her life with Elvis, is broadcast on ABC TV and becomes the highest-rated TV movie of 1987/88

Oct Lisa Marie marries musician Danny Keough

1989

NBC TV broadcasts *Elvis: Comeback 68* – a repeat of the programme broadcast on 3 December 1968, which *TV Guide* describes as the best rock performance ever on television

29 May Lisa Marie and her husband have a daughter, Danielle Riley

1990

May The first Elvis Awards ceremony is held in New York, and Eric Clapton is named Best Rock Guitarist

1992

A two-volume video collection is re-edited and broadcast as *Elvis, The Great Performances (Televised Version)*, with Priscilla hosting it from Graceland

A video, *Elvis, The Lost Performances*, is released, with unseen footage from the films of his concerts

22 Jan   A two-hour TV special, *The Elvis Conspiracy – The Elvis Files*, is broadcast; it alleges that Elvis went undercover for the FBI and is still alive

6 Apr   A postcard ballot is held to choose which image of Elvis is to be used on a US postage stamp; an image of a young Elvis is chosen. *US News & World Report* says that revenue from sales of the Elvis stamp is expected to reach $20 million. The stamp is released in January 1993 and becomes the best-selling stamp in US postal history

21 Oct   Lisa Marie and her husband have a second child, a boy named Benjamin Storm

1993

A video documentary, *Elvis in Hollywood*, is released, with footage from the first four films, out-takes and interviews with those involved at the time

A TV special, *America Comes to Graceland*, about Elvis's life and legacy, is broadcast in the US

1 Feb   Lisa Marie turns 25 and is entitled to take charge of her inheritance, but decides to found the Elvis Presley Trust to run the estate, with Priscilla and the National Bank of Commerce as co-trustees

1 Mar   *People* magazine estimates that Elvis's estate is now worth nearly $100 million

1994

Lisa Marie divorces Danny Keough

26 May   Michael Jackson and Lisa Marie are married in the Dominican Republic

1995

The 1956 recording of 'Heartbreak Hotel' is inducted into the NARAS Hall of Fame

1996

Lisa Marie divorces Michael Jackson

A virtual tour of Graceland is released on CD

1997

At the Mid-South Coliseum in Memphis, *Elvis in Concert 97* features Elvis on video accompanied live on stage by over 30 of his former band members and the Memphis Symphony Orchestra; a digitally remastered video is also shown, with Lisa Marie singing 'Don't Cry, Daddy' with Elvis

An official video tour, *Elvis Presley's Graceland*, is released

1998

The 1954 recording of 'That's All Right, Mama' is inducted into the NARAS Hall of Fame

Lisa Marie becomes owner and Chairman of the Board of Elvis Presley Enterprises, Inc, while Priscilla becomes Chairman of the Advisory Board

Elvis is posthumously inducted into the Country Music Hall of Fame

1999

The 1969 recording of 'Suspicious Minds' is inducted into the NARAS Hall of Fame

Nov–Jan   A two-part documentary, *He Touched Me: The Gospel Music of Elvis Presley*, is aired on TNN and the whole programme is also released as two videos

2001

21 Sept   'America The Beautiful', a special CD single featuring Elvis singing three songs, enters the *Billboard* Hot 100 singles sales chart at No. 8; it peaks at No. 6 for two weeks in November

Dec   Graceland is voted fourth Most Visited Historic House Museum in the United States, on the list compiled by the Almanac of Architecture and Design; Elvis is posthumously inducted into the Gospel Music Hall of Fame

2002

9 Jan   It is announced that the Vaughan-Bassett Furniture Company has gone into partnership with Elvis Presley Enterprises, Inc to manufacture an exclusive range of wood furniture to be known as the Elvis Presley Collection; the collection is launched later that year

Acknowledgments

All photographs in this book are reproduced by kind permission of Aquarius Collection Limited and Corbis.

Page 1 — Bettman, Corbis
Page 2 — Bettman, Corbis
Page 3 — Bettman, Corbis
Page 4 — Aquarius
Page 6 — Corbis
Page 8 — Aquarius
Page 9 — Bettman, Corbis

Chapter 1

Pages 10–11 — Bettman, Corbis
Page 12 — Bettman, Corbis
Page 14 — Bettman, Corbis
Page 15 — Aquarius
Page 16 — Corbis
Page 17 *(top)* — Aquarius
Page 17 *(bottom)* — Corbis
Page 18 — Corbis
Page 19 — Bettman, Corbis
Page 20 — Corbis
Page 21 — Corbis
Page 22 — Corbis
Page 23 *(top)* — Bettman, Corbis
Page 23 *(bottom)* — Bettman, Corbis
Page 24 — Aquarius
Page 25 — Aquarius
Pages 26–27 — Bettman, Corbis
Page 28 — Aquarius
Page 29 — Bettman, Corbis
Page 30 — Bettman, Corbis
Page 31 — Bettman, Corbis
Pages 32–33 — Bettman, Corbis
Page 34 — Bettman, Corbis
Page 35 — Bettman, Corbis
Page 36 *(top)* — Bettman, Corbis
Page 36 *(bottom)* — Bettman, Corbis
Page 37 — Bettman, Corbis
Page 38 — Bettman, Corbis
Page 39 *(top)* — Corbis
Page 39 *(bottom)* — Bettman, Corbis
Page 40 *(left)* — Hulton-Deutsch Collection, Corbis
Page 40 *(right)* — Corbis
Page 41 — Bettman, Corbis
Page 42 *(top)* — Corbis
Page 42 *(bottom)* — Corbis
Page 43 — Corbis
Page 44 — Twentieth Century Fox/ Aquarius
Page 45 *(top)* — Twentieth Century Fox/ Aquarius
Page 45 *(bottom)* — Twentieth Century Fox/ Aquarius
Page 46 — Twentieth Century Fox/ Aquarius
Page 47 *(top)* — Bettman, Corbis
Page 47 *(bottom)* — Corbis
Page 48 — Corbis
Page 49 — Corbis

Page 50 — Bettman, Corbis
Page 51 — Bettman, Corbis
Page 52 — Corbis
Page 53 *(top)* — Corbis
Page 53 *(bottom)* — Corbis
Page 54 — Corbis
Page 55 — Bettman, Corbis
Page 56 — Bettman, Corbis
Page 57 — Bettman, Corbis
Page 58 — Bettman, Corbis
Page 59 — Bettman, Corbis
Page 60 — Bettman, Corbis
Page 61 — Bettman, Corbis
Page 62 — Bettman, Corbis
Page 63 — Twentieth Century Fox/ Aquarius
Page 64 — Corbis
Page 65 *(top)* — Corbis
Page 65 *(bottom)* — Corbis
Page 66 — Corbis
Page 67 *(top)* — Corbis
Page 67 *(bottom)* — Corbis

Chapter 2

Pages 68–69 — Bettman, Corbis
Page 70 — Bettman, Corbis
Page 73 — Bettman, Corbis
Page 74 — Bettman, Corbis
Page 75 — Paramount/Aquarius
Page 76 *(top)* — Corbis
Page 76 *(bottom)* — Bettman, Corbis
Page 77 — Bettman, Corbis
Page 78 — Bettman, Corbis
Page 79 *(top)* — Bettman, Corbis
Page 79 *(bottom)* — Aquarius
Page 80 *(top)* — Bettman, Corbis
Page 80 *(bottom)* — Bettman, Corbis
Page 81 — MGM/Aquarius
Pages 82–83 — MGM/Aquarius
Page 84 — Bettman, Corbis
Page 85 *(top)* — Underwood and Underwood, Corbis
Page 85 *(bottom)* — Bettman, Corbis
Page 86 — Bettman, Corbis
Page 87 — Bettman, Corbis
Page 88 — Bettman, Corbis
Page 89 *(top)* — MGM/Aquarius
Page 89 *(bottom)* — Bettman, Corbis
Page 90 — Bettman, Corbis
Page 91 — Corbis
Page 92 — Bettman, Corbis
Page 93 *(top)* — Seattle Post-Intelligencer Collection; Museum of History and Industry, Corbis
Page 93 *(bottom)* — Corbis
Page 94 — Corbis
Page 95 — Corbis

Pages 96–97 — MGM/Aquarius
Page 98 *(top)* — Seattle Post-Intelligencer Collection; Museum of History and Industry, Corbis
Page 98 *(bottom)* — MGM/Aquarius
Page 99 — Bettman, Corbis

Chapter 3

Pages 100–101 — Bettman, Corbis
Page 102 — Bettman, Corbis
Page 104 — Paramount/Aquarius
Page 105 — Bettman, Corbis
Page 106 — Bettman, Corbis
Page 107 — Bettman, Corbis
Page 108 — Paramount/Aquarius
Page 109 — Bettman, Corbis
Page 110 — Bettman, Corbis
Page 111 — Bettman, Corbis
Page 112 — Bettman, Corbis
Page 113 — Bettman, Corbis
Page 114 — Bettman, Corbis
Page 115 — Bettman, Corbis
Page 116 — Bettman, Corbis
Page 117 *(left)* — Corbis
Page 117 *(right)* — Bettman, Corbis
Page 118 — Bettman, Corbis
Page 119 *(top)* — Bettman, Corbis
Page 119 *(bottom)* — Corbis
Pages 120–121 — Bettman, Corbis
Page 122 *(top)* — Bettman, Corbis
Page 122 *(bottom)* — Bettman, Corbis
Page 123 — Bettman, Corbis
Page 124 — Bettman, Corbis
Page 125 — Bettman, Corbis
Page 126 *(top)* — Bettman, Corbis
Page 126 *(bottom)* — Bettman, Corbis
Page 127 — Aquarius
Page 128 — Bettman, Corbis
Page 129 — Bettman, Corbis
Page 130 — Corbis
Page 131 — Bettman, Corbis
Page 132 — Bettman, Corbis
Page 133 — Bettman, Corbis
Page 134 — Corbis
Page 135 — Bettman, Corbis
Page 136 — Corbis
Page 137 — Bettman, Corbis
Page 138 — Bettman, Corbis
Page 139 — Bettman, Corbis
Page 140 — Bettman, Corbis
Page 141 — Corbis
Page 142 — Bettman, Corbis
Page 143 *(top)* — Bettman, Corbis
Page 143 *(bottom)* — Corbis
Page 144 *(top)* — Bettman, Corbis
Page 144 *(bottom)* — Corbis
Page 145 — Bettman, Corbis

Page 146 — Bettman, Corbis
Page 147 *(top)* — Bettman, Corbis
Page 147 *(bottom)* — Bettman, Corbis
Page 148 — Aquarius
Page 149 — Bettman, Corbis
Page 150 — Aquarius
Page 151 *(top)* — Bettman, Corbis
Page 151 *(bottom)* — Bettman, Corbis
Page 152 — Bettman, Corbis
Page 153 — Bettman, Corbis
Page 154 — Bettman, Corbis
Page 155 — Corbis
Page 156 *(top)* — Bettman, Corbis
Page 156 *(bottom)* — Bettman, Corbis
Page 157 — Bettman, Corbis
Page 158 — Corbis
Page 159 — Bettman, Corbis
Page 160 — Paramount/Aquarius
Page 161 — Bettman, Corbis
Pages 162–163 — Paramount/Aquarius
Page 164 — Paramount/Aquarius
Page 165 — Paramount/Aquarius
Page 166 — Paramount/Aquarius
Page 167 — Bettman, Corbis
Page 168 *(top)* — Bettman, Corbis
Page 168 *(bottom)* — Corbis
Page 169 — Paramount/Aquarius
Page 170 — Twentieth Century Fox/ Aquarius
Page 171 — Twentieth Century Fox/ Aquarius
Page 172 — Twentieth Century Fox/ Aquarius
Page 173 — Twentieth Century Fox/ Aquarius
Page 174 *(top)* — Twentieth Century Fox/ Aquarius
Page 174 *(bottom)* — Twentieth Century Fox/ Aquarius
Page 175 — Bettman, Corbis
Page 176 — Aquarius
Page 177 *(top)* — Bettman, Corbis
Page 177 *(bottom)* — Bettman, Corbis

Chapter 4

Pages 178–179 — Bettman, Corbis
Page 180 — Twentieth Century Fox/ Aquarius
Page 182 — Twentieth Century Fox/ Aquarius
Page 184 — Twentieth Century Fox/ Aquarius
Page 185 — Twentieth Century Fox/ Aquarius
Page 186 — Twentieth Century Fox/ Aquarius
Page 187 — Twentieth Century Fox/ Aquarius
Page 188 — Bettman, Corbis
Page 189 — Corbis

Page 190	Bettman, Corbis	Page 233	Bettman, Corbis	Page 276	Bettman, Corbis	Page 324 *(bottom)*	Bettman, Corbis
Page 191 *(top)*	Bettman, Corbis	Page 234	MGM/Aquarius	Page 277	Frank Carroll, Sygma	Page 325 *(top)*	Bettman, Corbis
Page 191 *(bottom)*	Hal B. Wallis, Paramount/Aquarius	Page 235	MGM/Aquarius	Page 278	Frank Carroll, Sygma	Page 325 *(bottom)*	Aquarius
Page 192	Bettman, Corbis	Page 236	MGM/Aquarius	Page 279 *(top)*	Frank Carroll, Sygma	Page 326	Bettman, Corbis
Page 193	Bettman, Corbis	Page 237	United Artists/Aquarius	Page 279 *(bottom)*	Frank Carroll, Sygma	Page 327 *(top)*	Bettman, Corbis
Page 194	Paramount/Aquarius	Pages 238–239	Bettman, Corbis	Page 280	Frank Carroll, Sygma	Page 327 *(bottom)*	Bettman, Corbis
Page 195 *(top)*	Bettman, Corbis	Page 240	Bettman, Corbis	Page 281	Frank Carroll, Sygma		
Page 195 *(bottom)*	Bettman, Corbis	Page 241	Bettman, Corbis			**Chapter 6**	
Page 196	United Artists/Aquarius	Page 242	Bettman, Corbis	**Chapter 5**		Pages 328–329	Bettman, Corbis
Page 197 *(top)*	Bettman, Corbis	Page 243	Bettman, Corbis	Pages 282–283	Bettman, Corbis	Page 330	Bettman, Corbis
Page 197 *(bottom)*	Bettman, Corbis	Page 244 *(top)*	Aquarius	Page 284	Spatz, Sygma	Page 332	Bettman, Corbis
Page 198 *(top)*	Bettman, Corbis	Page 244 *(bottom)*	Bettman, Corbis	Page 286	Bettman, Corbis	Page 333	Bettman, Corbis
Page 198 *(bottom)*	Paramount/Aquarius	Page 245	Bettman, Corbis	Page 287	MGM/Aquarius	Page 334 *(top)*	Bettman, Corbis
Page 199	Paramount/Aquarius	Page 246	MGM/Aquarius	Page 288	Sam Emerson, Sygma	Page 334 *(bottom)*	Bettman, Corbis
Page 200	Corbis	Page 247 *(top)*	MGM/Aquarius	Page 289	Sam Emerson, Sygma	Page 335	Bettman, Corbis
Page 201	Corbis	Page 247 *(bottom)*	MGM/Aquarius	Page 290	Sam Emerson, Sygma	Page 336 *(top)*	Bettman, Corbis
Page 202	Seattle Post-Intelligencer Collection; Museum of History and Industry, Corbis	Page 248	MGM/Aquarius	Page 291	MGM/Aquarius	Page 336 *(bottom)*	Roger Garwood and Trish Ainslie, Corbis
		Page 249	MGM/Aquarius	Pages 292–293	Bettman, Corbis	Page 337	Henry Diltz, Corbis
		Page 250	MGM/Aquarius	Page 294	Frank Carroll, Sygma	Page 338	Bettman, Corbis
Page 203	Seattle Post-Intelligencer Collection; Museum of History and Industry, Corbis	Page 251 *(top)*	MGM/Aquarius	Page 295	Frank Carroll, Sygma	Page 339	Franz-Marc Frei, Corbis
		Page 251 *(bottom)*	Bettman, Corbis	Page 296	Frank Carroll, Sygma	Page 340 *(top)*	Raymond Gehman, Corbis
		Page 252	Bettman, Corbis	Page 297 *(top)*	Frank Carroll, Sygma		
Page 204	MGM/Aquarius	Page 253	Bettman, Corbis	Page 297 *(bottom)*	Frank Carroll, Sygma	Page 340 *(bottom)*	Roger Garwood and Trish Ainslie, Corbis
Page 205	Paramount/Aquarius	Page 254 *(top)*	MGM/Aquarius	Page 298	Frank Carroll, Sygma	Page 341 *(top)*	Kevin Fleming, Corbis
Pages 206–207	Bettman, Corbis	Page 254 *(bottom)*	MGM/Aquarius	Page 299	Frank Carroll, Sygma	Page 341 *(bottom)*	Kevin Fleming, Corbis
Page 208	Bettman, Corbis	Page 255	MGM/Aquarius	Page 300 *(top)*	Corbis	Pages 342–343	Arthur Grace, Sygma
Page 209 *(top)*	Bettman, Corbis	Page 256	Bettman, Corbis	Page 300 *(bottom)*	Frank Carroll, Sygma	Page 343 *(inset)*	Henry Diltz, Corbis
Page 209 *(bottom)*	MGM/Aquarius	Page 257	Sygma	Page 301	Frank Carroll, Sygma	Page 344 *(top)*	Dave Bartruff, Corbis
Page 210	MGM/Aquarius	Page 258	Sygma	Page 302	Frank Carroll, Sygma	Page 344 *(bottom)*	Philip Gould, Corbis
Page 211	Aquarius	Page 259 *(top)*	Sygma	Page 303	Frank Carroll, Sygma	Page 345	Alain Nogues, Sygma
Page 212	Aquarius	Page 259 *(bottom)*	Sygma	Page 304 *(top)*	Frank Carroll, Sygma	Page 346 *(top)*	Jan Butchofsky-Houser, Corbis
Page 213	Bettman, Corbis	Page 260 *(top)*	MGM/Aquarius	Page 304 *(bottom)*	Frank Carroll, Sygma		
Pages 214–215	Bettman, Corbis	Page 260 *(bottom)*	MGM/Aquarius	Page 305	Frank Carroll, Sygma	Page 346 *(bottom)*	Raymond Gehman, Corbis
Page 216	Bettman, Corbis	Page 261	MGM/Aquarius	Pages 306–307	Korody, Sygma		
Page 217	Bettman, Corbis	Page 262	MGM/Aquarius	Page 308	Bettman, Corbis	Page 347	Kevin Fleming, Corbis
Page 218	Paramount/Aquarius	Page 263 *(top)*	MGM/Aquarius	Page 309 *(top)*	Bettman, Corbis		
Page 219 *(top)*	Paramount/Aquarius	Page 263 *(bottom)*	MGM/Aquarius	Page 309 *(bottom)*	Aquarius	**Bibliography and facts**	
Page 219 *(bottom)*	Allied Artists/Aquarius	Page 264 *(top)*	MGM/Aquarius	Page 310	Bettman, Corbis	Page 349	Corbis
Page 220 *(top)*	Allied Artists/Aquarius	Page 264 *(bottom)*	Bettman, Corbis	Page 311 *(top)*	Jeff Albertson, Corbis	Page 350	Aquarius
Page 220 *(bottom)*	Allied Artists/Aquarius	Page 265	MGM/Aquarius	Page 311 *(bottom)*	Jeff Albertson, Corbis	Pages 352–353	Paramount/Aquarius
Page 221	Allied Artists/Aquarius	Page 266	Aquarius	Page 312	Bettman, Corbis	Page 354	Paramount/Aquarius
Page 222	Allied Artists/Aquarius	Page 267 *(top)*	National General, Aquarius	Page 313 *(top)*	Jeff Albertson, Corbis	Page 355	MGM/Aquarius
Page 223 *(top)*	Allied Artists/Aquarius			Page 313 *(bottom)*	Bettman, Corbis	Page 356	Aquarius
Page 223 *(bottom)*	Allied Artists/Aquarius	Page 267 *(bottom)*	National General, Aquarius	Page 314 *(top)*	Bettman, Corbis	Page 357	Corbis
Page 224 *(top)*	Allied Artists/Aquarius			Page 314 *(bottom)*	Bettman, Corbis		
Page 224 *(bottom)*	Allied Artists/Aquarius	Page 268	National General, Aquarius	Page 315	Bettman, Corbis	**Chronology**	
Page 225	Allied Artists/Aquarius			Page 316	Bettman, Corbis	Page 358	Aquarius
Page 226	Allied Artists/Aquarius	Page 269 *(top)*	MGM/Aquarius	Page 317	Aquarius	Page 362	Aquarius
Page 227	Allied Artists/Aquarius	Page 269 *(bottom)*	MGM/Aquarius	Page 318 *(top)*	MGM/Aquarius	Page 369	Paramount/Aquarius
Page 228	MGM/Aquarius	Page 270	Aquarius	Page 318 *(bottom)*	Bettman, Corbis	Page 373	Corbis
Page 229	United Artists/Aquarius	Page 271	Aquarius	Page 319	Bettman, Corbis	Page 378	Corbis
Page 230	Aquarius	Page 272	Bettman, Corbis	Page 320	Bettman, Corbis	Page 381	Corbis
Page 231	Bettman, Corbis	Page 273	Bettman, Corbis	Page 321 *(top)*	Aquarius		
Page 232 *(top)*	MGM/Aquarius	Page 274	Bettman, Corbis	Page 321 *(bottom)*	Bettman, Corbis		
Page 232 *(bottom)*	Bettman, Corbis	Page 275 *(top)*	Corbis	Page 322	Bettman, Corbis		
		Page 275 *(bottom)*	Universal/Aquarius	Page 323	Lynn Goldsmith, Corbis		
				Page 324 *(top)*	Bettman, Corbis		

Every effort has been made to ensure that the copyright details shown are correct, but if there are any inaccuracies, please contact the publisher.